"The soul hears the Word
pline of 'creative listening' ı
book, *Greater Things.*"
—*Michael Card, award winning artist, songwriter, and author*

"As it says in Proverbs 25:11, 'Like apples of gold in settings of silver, is a word spoken at the proper time,' Pastor David Kim's words have always been like apples of God in settings of silver whenever I read them. God has given him the gift of being able to use words as a soothing salve for a parched soul. Next to the Word of God itself, David's writings are perfect for daily reading."
—*Rev. Cory Ishida, Pastor Emeritus of Evergreen Baptist Church in Los Angeles*

"Pastor David Kim is a gifted writer and poet with amazing insights given to him by God, especially during the pandemic. *Greater Things* radiates hope from beginning to end and will be a great source of encouragement and blessing for all who read it."
—Andy Pearce, *Southern California Regional Director, International Students, Inc. Ministries*

"David Kim has captured the times and the deepest feelings of humanity in his words and meter. His words are a much needed source of understanding, insight, and peace in difficult times."
—*Chris Stanton, Missionary and founder of Mission Bridge*

"Need encouragement? A boost to your faith? Dive into David Kim's honest, personal, faith-filled devotionals and poems. It is a daily dose of truth and fire."
—*Rev. Doug Schaupp, National Director of Evangelism, InterVarsity, Author of Breaking the Huddle*

"In *Greater Things*, Pastor David Kim directs us to God's promises in scripture. Through poetic prayers and faith responses, he inspires us to greater hope and faith in Jesus and His presence and power at work in and around us. If you're struggling with fear or discouragement, or your heart just longs to be infused with joy and grateful praise to our great God, you will find this book water for your thirsty soul!"

—*Dr. Bill and Dr. Kristi Gaultiere, founders of Soul Shepherding and authors of* Journey of the Soul: A Practical Guide to Emotional and Spiritual Growth

"I appreciate Pastor David Kim's heart and soul in these devotional poems. His love and connection to God are expressed so passionately and honestly. These give us a way to connect to God when we don't have our own words to express our soul's need for hope, faith, and love. I love that each devotional starts with scripture that sets the theme of the poem, then his pastoral words, and then the poem. I look forward to using these in my times to connect with Jesus!"

—*Sandy Lee Schaupp, Spiritual Director of staff with InterVarsity Christian Fellowship*

Greater Things

David Kim

RIVER BIRCH PRESS

Daphne, Alabama

ISBN 978-1-956365-02-3 (print)
ISBN 978-1-956365-03-0 (e-book)

For Worldwide Distribution
Printed in the U.S.A.

River Birch Press
P.O. Box 868, Daphne, AL 36526

TABLE OF CONTENTS

Introduction

God has *Greater Things* in store for your life! He has called you to go from "Faith to Faith" and "Glory to Glory"! The global Covid-19 pandemic brought the whole world to a standstill. Yet, in the midst of it all, God was on the throne, making all things work together for the good of those who love Him and are called according to His purpose (Romans 8:28).

Greater Things!—a book of 120 devotional poems—is a book of hope. Like the psalmist, David, writing these poems has helped me process the deep things in my heart before the Lord. The Lord has met me in writing them and has brought great encouragement to my soul. My prayer is that they may bring faith, hope, and love to your hearts. To God be the glory for the *Greater Things* that He will do in our lives!

I have divided the devotional poems into three sections: Hope, Faith, and Love, based on the 1 Corinthians 13:13, "Three things will last forever—faith, hope, and love—and the greatest of these is love." I started with Hope, for this is what I believe we need first diring the times in which we are living!

I dedicate this book to the Lord Jesus Christ,
who saved my soul when I called on His Name in 1988
at 18 years of age. He has been faithfully leading and guiding my life
over these past 30+ years since then, including during this crazy time of
the Covid 19 pandemic. The Lord literally woke me up in the middle of
the night and downloaded to my heart and mind many of the poems in
this book! Thank you, Lord, for Your inspiration and Your Presence in
my life!

I also dedicate this book to my wife, Sharon,
who has been my life partner for the past 29 years.
So thankful for her love, support, and full partnership
in the ministry over all these years.
Our best days are ahead of us!

HOPE

And this hope will not lead to disappointment. For we know how dearly God loves us, because he has given us the Holy Spirit to fill our hearts with his love (Romans 5:5 NLT).

How we need God's hope in our lives! Not the wishful thinking worldly hope, but the Rock of Jesus solid hope of God! God's hope does not disappoint! I pray that these poems about hope will help you encounter the God of hope!

→ 1 ←

"The glory of this present house will be greater than the glory of the former house," says the Lord Almighty. "And in this place I will grant peace," declares the Lord Almighty (Haggai 2:9 NIV).

God has greater things in store for you! The glory of your present house will be greater than the glory of your former house! The Bible speaks of going from "faith to faith" and "glory to glory"—from one level of faith and glory to the next. Live in the expectation of the greater things that the Lord has in store for your life.

Greater Things!

Greater things
You have in store!
Eternal God
In You there's more!

No ear has heard
No eye has seen
What You'll unfold
The glorious things

Revealed in Your Word
Promised to us!
We believe
In You we trust!

Jesus said
We'd do the same
Miracles
In His name!

Yes and amen!
Lord let it be
Greater things
Done through me!

✢ 2 ✣

Very truly I tell you, whoever believes in Me will do the works I have been doing, and they will do even greater things than these, because I am going to the Father (John 14:12 NIV).

Greater things! The Lord will do greater things in His disciples than He did in His ministry while He was on earth! Jesus is the same yesterday, today, and forever (John 13:8). The same Jesus who worked miracles 2000 years ago now does His miracles through His disciple—that's you and me! Lay hold of this promise today, asking God to do greater things in your life!

Greater Things! (PART TWO)

Greater things
You will do!
Unbelief
I bid adieu!

The blind will see
The deaf will hear
Kingdom coming
In higher gear.

Increase my faith
Lord, I believe!
By faith Your promises
I receive!

Impossible things
Coming true
From the Gospels
We take our cue.

Greater things
Coming to pass
Testimonies
We'll broadcast!

✈ 3 ✦

And we know that God causes everything to work together for the good of those who love God and are called according to his purpose for them (Romans 8:28 NLT).

God works all things together for good! What an amazing promise from our heavenly Father! This brings much hope in the midst of these crazy times we've been living in. He takes it all—the good, the bad, and the ugly—and brings it together for our good and for His glory! I don't know how He does it, but He does it! And thank God that He does!

All Things Work Together for Good

God makes all things
Work together for our good
A promise I've lived by
On which I have stood.

All of my faults
All my mistakes
All of the things
That have brought heartache.

He brings them together
And works them for good
The Heavenly Mechanic
Working under our hood.

Shaping us into
The likeness of Christ.
He's making a masterpiece
His work is precise.

So trust in His working
Trust in His plan
For He's got the whole world
In His good hands!

☩ 4 ☩

And this hope will not lead to disappointment. For we know how dearly God loves us, because he has given us the Holy Spirit to fill our hearts with his love (Romans 5:5 NLT).

Hope is rising! God's hope does not disappoint us. Worldly hope will surely let us down. We have a God who is all powerful and all loving. He is for us and not against us. Therefore, we never lose hope for this God is always with us. Grab hold of the hope that comes from knowing the God of hope today!

Hope Is Rising

Hope is rising
In the air
God is working
Everywhere!

Birds are singing
Chirps of praise
Feel the warmth
Of the sun's rays.

Winter snow
Melting away
Flowers blooming
Full array.

Hope is stirring
In our hearts
Getting ready
New season starts.

God is moving
In this hour
Hope is real
Feel its power!

⇥ 5 ⇤

Enlarge the place of your tent, stretch your tent curtains wide, do not hold back; lengthen your cords, strengthen your stakes (Isaiah 54:2 NIV)

The Lord is enlarging your tent! He is calling you to expand your heart capacity to receive and experience His love. He is also expanding your hand capacity—your influence and reach for His Kingdom. The Lord is pouring out His Spirit upon you in a fresh way and enlarging you to do the good works that He has called you to do!

Enlarge My Tent

Enlarge my tent, Lord
This is my prayer
More capacity
For others' care.

Enlarge my vision, Lord
Help me to see
The world as You see it
From eternity.

Enlarge my faith, Lord
Help me to believe
All that You say
I want to receive.

Enlarge my heart, Lord
Help me to feel
What breaks Your heart
To know it for real.

Enlarge my tent, Lord
I embrace Your plan
Praying for increase
Your glory expand!

✦ 6 ✦

But we all, with unveiled faces, beholding as in a mirror the glory of the Lord, are being transformed into the same image from glory to glory, just as by the Spirit of the Lord (2 Corinthians 3:18 NKJV).

Transformation! You are being transformed into the likeness of the Lord from glory to glory! You are not the same person you were when you first started your journey with the Lord. As you spend time in His Presence, you are changed. You cannot be in His presence and stay the same. Lord, transform me more and more to be like Jesus!

Glory to Glory!

From faith to faith
And glory to glory
That's how He rolls
Unfolds His story.

Alpha and Omega
Beginning and the End
He wins the battle
In the Book He's penned.

Make my life
A testimony
Rid me of
The world's baloney!

Greater depth
In my walk with You
Beholding beauty
In what is true.

Moving forward
Full steam ahead!
Filled with power
Spirit led!

⇥ 7 ⇤

He put a new song in my mouth, a hymn of praise to our God.
Many will see and fear the Lord and put their trust in Him
(Psalms 40:3 NIV).

The Lord has given you a new song to sing to Him! A song of
hope, a song of freedom! As you sing our new song, others will
hear and join you! Soon it will become a choir that will sing
choruses of testimonies that declare the wonders of the Lord!

New Song!

Sing a new song
To the Lord
Voices raised
In one accord.

A song of hope
For today
Been through the fire
Been through the fray.

You placed our feet
Upon a rock.
New doors
Will be unlocked!

New melody
New harmony
All the people
In unity!

A song of JOY
I will rejoice.
In You, my Lord
I've made my choice!

✦ 8 ✦

To all who mourn in Israel, he will give a crown of beauty for ashes, a joyous blessing instead of mourning, festive praise instead of despair (Isaiah 61:3 NLT)

Hope is in the air! Out of the ashes of my troubles, I will arise! Troubles cause you to dig deeper in your walk with God and also birth a deeper sense of hope. We become a people refined and ready to do the will of God. A people with a fresh sense of purpose and a fresh zeal to serve! Lord, release Your people into the earth to shine forth Your glory!

Out of the Ashes

Out of the ashes
We will arise!
Showing His beauty
Flying like butterflies.

Out of our pains
Our griefs and our sorrows,
The Lord gives us hope
For better tomorrows.

Beauty for ashes
Hope for despair
The Lord is our healer
He truly cares.

Romans 8:28
A promise to hold
All things together
For good will unfold.

He is the Redeemer
Makes all things beautiful.
Our lives will become
Lovely and bountiful!

↣ 9 ↢

He brought me out into a spacious place; He rescued me because He delighted in me (Psalm 18: 19 NIV)

Praise God for His miracles! In Nov 2016, I had an aortic dissection and rupture with emergency open heart surgery. The Lord miraculously saved my life. After my dissection, I experienced depression and confusion and was going to quit the ministry. Right after my dissection, the Lord gave to me and my wife, Sharon, the verse Psalm 18:19—"He brought me out into a spacious place; he rescued me because he delighted in me." I didn't experience this spacious place until Easter 2018, when the Lord brought a spiritual breakthrough in my life. Glory to God!

A Spacious Place

You've made for me
A spacious place
A place of grace
A sacred space!

To run and play
Let down my guard
To freely roam
In God's backyard!

A place to be
A place to be still
A place to discern
God's good and perfect will

A place to hang
With my friends
Eternal place
That never ends!

Lord You are
My spacious place!
Here I meet you
Face to face!

✣ 10 ✣

But You, O Lord, are a shield about me, my glory, and the lifter of my head. I cried aloud to the Lord, and He answered me from His holy hill (Psalm 3:3-4 NKJV).

I love the Psalms of David! So real, so honest, so filled with the full range of human emotion. In Psalm 3, King David was being driven from his throne by a rebellion led by his own son Absalom. How painful it is to be betrayed, especially by someone you deeply love. In his despair, David cries out to the Lord who is "the lifter of his head." As the Lord met David in his dark hour, He will meet you in your time of difficulty. May the Lord be the lifter of your head today!

Lifter of My Head

Trouble abounds everywhere
Trouble lies within me.
Lifter of my head,
Hear my desperate plea.

There are no easy answers
To be found
I've looked and queried
All around.

At the end
Of my rope
Is the place
Where I find hope.

Lifter of my head
Rescued me from dread
Dying in my stead
Rising from the dead.

Praise the Lord
O my soul
Lifter of my head
I extol!

✦ 11 ✦

O God, please come and save us again; bring us your break-through-victory! (Psalm 118:25 Passion)

Easter is the greatest breakthrough victory in human history! Jesus conquered sin and death for you and for me! Experience His breakthrough today! If you have never accepted Christ into your life, today is the day! Call on His name, and you too will experience this amazing spiritual breakthrough of salvation in your life!

Breakthrough!

Greatest breakthrough ever
Jesus defeated death!
Jesus breathed again
After taking His last breath!

Breakthru of breakthru
Jesus rose again
Gives us all a Living Hope
Can you say Amen?

On the cross He died
Took on all our sin
Suffered for you and me
Took it on the chin.

"It is finished" He cried out
The curtain tore in two,
Giving access to all
Not just for the few.

Hallelujah to the Lamb
Who overcame the grave
His breakthru is for all
For all He's come to save!

✤ 12 ✤

Yet even in the midst of all these things, we triumph over them all, for God has made us to be more than conquerors, and His demonstrated love is our glorious victory over everything! (Romans 8:37 Passion)

You are an overcomer! You will face all kinds of trials. The devil throws everything at you, including the kitchen sink. Jesus told you it would be like this. And He also told you to "Be of good cheer, for I have overcome the world!" (John 16:33) Through Christ, you are more than a conqueror! You are an overcomer!

Overcomers!

An overcomer
Is what I am!
By Your Spirit
All things I can.

Do the impossible
With faith in You
Seeing things
From Kingdom view.

No weapon formed
Against me will
Ever prosper
So I can chill!

Knowing that
You're always with me
When in trouble
You come swiftly!

Overcomer
Is my name!
Testimonies
I'll proclaim!

13

✢ 13 ✢

Therefore, since we are surrounded by so great a cloud of witnesses, let us also lay aside every weight, and sin which clings so closely, and let us run with endurance the race that is set before us (Hebrews 12:1 ESV).

"You got this!" Hear the cloud of witnesses shouting encouragement as you run the race marked before you! Encouragement from the heavenly cloud gives you strength and courage to keep on keeping on. Those who have gone before us remind us that this race is doable and that your race is almost complete! You got this!

Cloud of Witnesses

Cloud of witnesses
Cheering us on!
Those who've run their race
And to heaven have gone.

"Keep on running!
You're almost there!"
Strengthening me
In this warfare.

Abraham and Moses
Faces in the cloud
You got this!
Make us all proud!

Mom and Dad are there
Cheering from above
You can do this, son!
We're sending you our love.

Looking to Jesus
As I run my race
Keep my eyes fixed
My fuel is His grace!

✦ 14 ✦

There is more than enough room in My Father's home. If this were not so, would I have told you that I am going to prepare a place for you? When everything is ready, I will come and get you, so that you will always be with Me where I am (John 14:2-3 NLT).

Jesus is preparing a place for you in heaven. How exciting and awesome is that! A place where there are no more tears, no more suffering or death. This world and this life on earth is only your temporary home. You can live each day with heaven in mind for soon, and very soon, His disciples will join Him there!

Heaven!

Heaven is my home
My permanent address
Something to look forward to
When I get depressed.

Jesus is there,
Preparing a place for me.
Can't wait to go there
With my own eyes to see!

No more tears and no more pain
A place of full shalom.
No more war, no more disease
Where I am fully known.

Better than Eden
Where we'll forever dwell
Singing on repeat
The song, "It is well!"

Spirit in my heart
A piece of heaven here
Eternity has begun
Our new life frontier!

✥ 15 ✥

Arise, shine, for your light has come, and the glory of the Lord has risen upon you (Isaiah 60:1 ESV).

Arise, people of God! The Lord shines upon you; His glory has risen upon you! In times of trial and chaos, you can rise above your circumstances and soar in His presence. You will mount up on wings like eagles. Wait in His presence. Let His Spirit Wind fill your sails and rise with Him!

I Will Rise

I will rise
On eagle's wings
In my times
Of worshipping.

In Your presence
I will soar
Serving You
Is never a chore.

I'll rise above
This earthly realm
I'll spread my sails
You at the helm.

Trusting Jesus
Full speed ahead!
Breaking barriers
Spirit led.

Seated in
Heavenly places
Glory shining
On our faces!

✦ 16 ✦

Then he said to me, "Prophesy to these bones and say to them, 'Dry bones, hear the word of the Lord! This is what the Sovereign Lord says to these bones: I will make breath enter you, and you will come to life'" (Ezekiel 37:4-5 NIV).

Dry bones, come alive in the name of the Lord! The Lord has called you to speak to the dry bones of our day—the lost souls, the prodigal sons and daughters, those bound up by the adversary. You have the authority to prophesy in Jesus' name and to call forth the things of the Kingdom into being! Hallelujah!

Prophesy

Prophesy to the dry bones!
They will come alive.
In the name of Jesus
You will live and thrive!

The Word of God in power
Strongholds are destroyed
Will accomplish its purpose
Will never return void.

Calling into being
Things that once were not
Creative miracles
Come forth from His thoughts.

"Let there be light" and there was light!
The power of His Word
Spoken by His people
Cancers are now cured.

Prophesy to the dry bones!
His mighty Word proclaims!
Raise up a mighty army
With hearts that are aflame!

⇥ 17 ⇤

The wind blows where it wishes, and you hear the sound of it, but cannot tell where it comes from and where it goes. So is everyone who is born of the Spirit (John 3:8 NKJV).

The fresh wind of God is blowing! You cannot see the wind, but there is clear evidence where the wind has blown. So it is with the wind of the Spirit. The wind of the Spirit blows over you, bringing refreshing and renewal. You are changed by the wind of the Holy Spirit. Fresh wind of the Spirit, blow over me today!

Fresh Wind

Fresh wind from heaven
Blow o'er the earth
Hovering over us
Waiting to give birth.

Bring forth revival!
Salvation and more!
Bring resurrection
On eagles' wings we'll soar!

Blow away fear
Stale things in our lives.
In this time of trial
You cause our souls to thrive

Breathe in new vision
Purpose that's from You,
Lead us in Your calling
Kingdom rendezvous!

Fresh wind how we need you!
Fill us breath of God!
Exhaling forth Your praises
Your great works we applaud!

✢ 18 ✢

Be still, and know that I am God. I will be exalted among the nations, I will be exalted in the earth! (Psalm 46:10 NKJV)

Be still! There is so much craziness all around. Every day another shoe drops. Violence, fear, racism, anxiety—this is the air we breathe. Take a step back and be still. Breathe in. Breathe out. The Lord is near. He is in control!

Be Still

Take a moment
To be still
In His presence
Wait until

Peace flows down
Into your heart
His shalom
He will impart

Peace that passes
Understanding
Breathe it in
It is expanding.

Guard your heart
And your mind
Holy Spirit
Will remind

That God is fully
In control
In His love
Be made whole.

✣ 19 ✣

Create in me a clean heart, O God. Renew a loyal spirit within me (Psalms 51:10 NLT).

Only the Lord can change my heart! The Lord can change my hardened heart into soft clay. The Lord cleanses our sinful hearts to hearts that are made clean and whole. Oh how we need the Lord to continually work in and on our hearts. May our hearts be made into the likeness of Christ!

Change My Heart, O God

Change my heart, O God
Make it ever true
I've sung this song a million times
I sing today anew.

Turn this heart of stone
Into a heart of flesh.
I need You to revive
I need You to refresh.

Battles thru the day
Arrows fly by night
Jesus come and save
Come and help me fight!

This battle for my heart
Wages day by day.
Daily surrender
Is the only way.

Change my heart, O God
Lord, I come to You
My heart is fully Yours
You will see me through!

☩ 20 ☩

As iron sharpens iron, so a friend sharpens a friend (Proverbs
27:17 NLT)

We truly need one another! To comfort one another, to strengthen
one another, to encourage one another, to challenge one another.
Thank God for His family that we can be iron sharpening iron to
one another. No believer stands alone; we stand together in the
Lord!

As Iron Sharpens Iron

As iron sharpens iron
We sharpen one another
For we are family
Sisters and brothers!

We speak the truth in love
Bringing to the light
We need accountability!
In this spiritual fight.

The devil doesn't play
Wants to kill and destroy
We got each other's back
We're a heavenly convoy!

Linking up our shields
Bringing out our swords
Speaking forth His truth
Declaring Living Words.

We're all in this together
No one stands alone
We need one another
We're never on our own!

✤ 21 ✤

This means that anyone who belongs to Christ has become a new person. The old life is gone; a new life has begun! (2 Corinthians 5:17 NLT).

When you come to Christ, you become a new creation in Him! The old has gone, the new has come! I think that the transformation of the butterfly is a perfect picture of our new life in Christ. We once were dingy caterpillars, and when we accepted Jesus, He transformed us into glorious butterflies! Glory to God!

Butterflies!

I love butterflies!
Miracles in the air!
Showing God's beauty
His glory they declare!

Transformed from chrysalis
Waiting to be born
Bursting from cocoons
The earth they do adorn.

They remind me of our lives
When we are born again,
The old has gone, the new has come!
To life that never ends.

Flying forth in freedom
Once bound to the ground
Beautiful and delicate
God's creativity abounds!

Come be a butterfly!
Experience God's transformation!
In Christ we are free
We are a new creation!

✧ 22 ✧

I have told you these things so that you will be filled with My joy. Yes, your joy will overflow! (John 15:11 NLT).

There is joy in the journey! "Joy in the Journey" is the name of one of my favorite songs written by one of my favorite artists, Michael Card. The words go- "There is a joy in the journey, there's a light we can love on the way. There is a wonder and wildness to life, and freedom for those who obey." This joy comes from the Lord; the joy in the journey comes from being with the Lord!

Joy in the Journey

There's joy in the journey
Laughter on the way
Even in the valley
The Son shines His rays.

Of light and love upon us
Warming up our hearts
He's a shield about us
From the fiery darts.

When the enemy comes
In like a flood
I praise the name of Jesus
There's power in the blood.

Your Spirit is my compass
My real life GPS
Often says, "Recalculating"
Cleaning up my mess!

You are my journey
My final destiny.
On time but rarely early
I put my hope in Thee!

⇢ 23 ⇠

Then God blessed them and said, "Be fruitful and multiply. Fill the earth and govern it. Reign over the fish in the sea, the birds in the sky, and all the animals that scurry along the ground" (Genesis 1:28 NLT).

Be fruitful and multiply! The first command to multiply was given to Adam and Eve in the Garden. This command to multiply was repeated in Jesus' Great Commission to make disciples of all nations. The Lord will take your life and multiply it for His glory. Lord, take our lives, our talents, our treasures and multiply them for Your Kingdom!

Multiply

Multiply
Your works, O Lord
In my life
I will record

The record of
Your faithfulness
In my failures
And success.

Multiply
Your love thru me
A sign to Jesus
I want to be.

For others to know
The One I know
That there is more to life
Than living YOLO

Multiply
My life, O Lord
Making disciples
Who obey Your Word!

✣ 24 ✣

But what was sown on good, rich soil represents the one who hears and fully embraces the message of the kingdom. Their lives bear good fruit—some yield a harvest of thirty, sixty, even one hundred times as much as was sown (Matthew 13:23 Passion).

Lord, make my heart into good soul! The parable of the Sower is such a true-to-life picture of reality. Jesus, the Sower, sows His seeds into the four different types of heart soils. Only one of the soils bears good fruit. Lord, make our hearts into the good soil that will receive Your Word and bear fruit for Your glory!

The Sower

The Sower sows the seed
Into the many soils
The devil comes to steal,
Destroy, and to spoil.

Protect the seed You've sown
Deep down in my heart
Let Your Word take root
May its life impar.t

Freedom to my soul
Your Words are life to me
Planted in my life
They will become a tree.

The Sower tends His garden,
Getting rid of rocks
Taking out the weeds
Preparing the stalks.

To bear much holy fruit
Fruit that will remain
Turning all the earth
To fruitful Kingdom terrain!

✦ 25 ✦

If My people, who are called by My name, will humble them-selves and pray and seek My face and turn from their wicked ways, then I will hear from heaven, and I will forgive their sin and will heal their land (2 Chronicles 7:14 NIV).

Heal our land, Lord! There is so much division and injustice in our land. We, as believers, must lament and speak out against violence and injustice. And pray for the healing of our broken, divided country. Healing of our land is possible only through the love of Jesus!

Heal Our Land

Anger and sadness
Equally fill my soul
This anti-Asian hate
Leaves a gaping hole.

Perpetually seen as foreigners
In this place called home
This is our country too
We're American to the bone.

The model minority myth
Perpetuates the lie
Of white supremacy
Causing people to die.

Lord please heal our hearts
Lord please heal our land
In Your love and grace
We ALL take a stand.

To end this ugly hate
It starts with the One
Loving our neighbor
It's how this battle's won.

✤ 26 ✦

"What do you want Me to do for you?" Jesus asked (Mark 10:51 NLT).

God will give you the desire of your heart! Jesus asks you the same question today, "What do you want Me to do for you?" What is your heart's desire? Dig deeper into your heart to see what deep desire lies within. Jesus wants for you to bring your desires to Him. He will bring them forth in your life! Praise His name!

Desire

Deep down inside
Lies the desire
Burning within
Set me on fire!

If I could do anything,
What would it be?
When the haze disappears,
What do I see?

Before I was born
You called me to do
The works You've prepared
In advance You knew.

Burning fire
Inside my bones
Crying out
My spirit groans.

To do Your will
Is my desire
Getting hotter
Soaring higher!

⇜ 27 ⇝

Then He said to them, "Follow Me, and I will make you fishers of men." They immediately left their nets and followed Him (Matthew 4:19-20 NKJV).

I love to fish! It is one of my favorite hobbies. Jesus calls you to fish not for fish but for people. The joy of bringing someone into the Kingdom is far greater than reeling in any fish! What an awesome adventure that Jesus calls you to—fishing for people and bringing them to the Lord!

Fisher of Men

Follow Me and be
A fisher of men,
Leading people to
Be born again!

Bringing Good News
There's salvation in My name
Healing the sick
This is why I came.

Letting others know
That I can set them free
Living out Your faith
So people can see Me.

Showing by example
The love that I've shown you
Loving unconditionally
Seeing people's value.

Respond to the call
To be fishers of men!
Will you say yes?
Will you say amen?

✣ 28 ✣

We have this hope as an anchor for the soul, firm and secure. It enters the inner sanctuary behind the curtain (Hebrews 6:19 NIV).

Hope is oxygen for the soul! Hope allows us to breathe, especially in difficult and trying circumstances. Worldly hope can be mere wishful thinking. Biblical hope in God is sure and certain for it is based on the unshakeable promises of God!

The Anchor of HOPE

The anchor of hope
Is sure and certain
Leads me thru
The inner curtain.

Advent season
Full of hope!
Awaiting Messiah
God is Dope!

Confident expectancy
Hope defined
All God's promises
Jesus signed!

Wishful thinking
Does not apply
Jesus' hope
Won't be denied!

Come Lord Jesus!
Our hope's in You!
With your hope
We'll make it thru!

⊹ 29 ⊱

For the joy of the Lord is your strength (Nehemiah 8:10 NIV)

His joy is your strength! His joy gives you energy, the spring in your step. This joy springs from within; it is not dependent upon the changing circumstances around you. This joy comes from Jesus, our joyful Savior. May the Lord fill you with fresh joy today, and may that joy strengthen you in all you do.

The Joy of Jesus!

The joy of Jesus!
In every season
Good News for ALL!
You're the Reason!

Shepherds were
The first to know
In Excelsis
De-o!

Greatest news
Known to man!
For every tribe
And every clan!

Immanuel!
God is with us!
The World's Minus
Turned to PLUS!

Joy, Joy, Joy!
Jump up for joy!
Tell the world
It's a BOY!

✦ 30 ✦

Glory to God in the highest heaven, and on earth peace to those on whom His favor rests (Luke 2:14 NIV)

The Prince of Peace has come to peace on earth! This peace was accomplished on the cross, where peace between God and sinful man was established. This is Good News! You can have peace with God! You are at peace with God! And His peace fills your life each day!

Peace on Earth!

Peace on earth to everyone
The Prince of Peace is here!
Hatred, strife, and all ill will
Will soon disappear!

Peace with God made on the Cross
Our sins have been paid for!
The curse on man has been redeemed
The devil wins no more!

Receive His peace, a gift that's free!
A peace to live and know
A peace that passes understanding
A peace that won't plateau.

Spread His peace to all your friends
This Good News must be shared
The Greatest News of all time
Nothing can compare!

✣ 31 ✣

Where is the One who has been born king of the Jews? We saw His star when it rose and have come to worship Him (Matthew 2:2 NIV).

The King is here! The magi came from the East to worship the King, the Messiah. When they encountered the King, they were filled with joy and worshipped. Let us come and adore Him. Offer your life to Him as a living sacrifice—this is your acceptable worship!

The King Is Here!

No more fear!
The King is here!
Immanuel's come
Be of good cheer!

Your Kingdom come,
Your will be done!
Kingdom of darkness
Overrun!

A reign of justice
A reign of peace
A reign where captives
Are released!

The King is here!
The birth of Christ!
Greatest treasure
Pearl of great price!

The King is here!
The King is here!
Changing the
Whole atmosphere!

✤ 32 ✦

As the deer pants for streams of water, so my soul pants for you, my God. My soul thirsts for God, for the living God. When can I go and meet with God? (Psalms 42:1-2 NIV)

Our hearts long for God! Our souls thirst for His Presence. God has created you with a heart that longs for Him. He has placed in your heart longings that can only be fulfilled by Him. Nothing else, no one else can fully satisfy your heart. Take time today to have your longings met in the love of God.

Longing

Longings deep within my soul
Buried in my heart
Take time to come to surface
Quickly they depart.

Longing to be deeply known
A longing to be loved
Part of being human
It's what we're all made of.

Hearts are restless till they find
Their full rest in Thee
God-shaped vacuum in my soul
Without You, life is empty.

Longing to live fully
Without fear and regret
Long to be free
From my sins and debts.

Jesus, You're my longing
My longings are fulfilled
In You I find belonging
On You my life I build!

✣ 33 ✦

But when the fullness of the time had come, God sent forth His Son, born of a woman, born under the law, to redeem those who were under the law, that we might receive the adoption as sons (Galatians 4:4-5 NKJV).

God's timing is perfect! In the fullness of time, He sent His Son to the earth to seek and save the lost. Everyone has a time to encounter the Lord. Don't miss it. He is continually seeking after each one of us, like the Good Shepherd who left the 99 sheep to rescue the one. Lay hold of Him today!

The Fullness of Time

It was the perfect moment
Fruit ripened on the vine
The coming of Messiah
In the fullness of time

Four hundred years of silence
God chose to be still
Great anticipation
Building up until

Mary heard the angel
You shall be with Child
This Child shall be the Savior
Through Him we're reconciled

Each one has their moment
Their own fullness of time
When the Savior comes
And says "You are mine."

Now is the time
The time to be saved!
Open up your heart
Receive the gift He gave!

☙ 34 ❧

Then Samuel took a stone and set it up between Mizpah and Shen. He named it Ebenezer, saying, "Thus far the Lord has helped us" (1 Samuel 7:12 NIV).

God has helped you thus far! Take time today to reflect upon your life and remember how He has worked in your life. Surely God has helped you. Set up a stone of Ebenezer and give God the praise for His faithfulness.

Halftime

Halftime's the time
To take a rest
To get perspective
To catch your breath.

To think about
The half before
To prepare yourself
For the half in store.

To hear from Coach
X's and O's
Fresh game plan
From the One who knows.

Covid crisis
Like halftime
Pressing pause
Fresh wind to find.

Halftime period
Almost done!
The very BEST
Is yet to come!

✢ 35 ✤

There is a river whose streams make glad the city of God, the holy place where the Most High dwells (Psalm 46:4 NIV).

The river is here! I remember singing the Vineyard song, "The River of God" at one of our church retreats. The whole church made a train, and we were dancing and singing in the sanctuary. We were all like little kids frollicking and playing in God's wide river. There is joy in the river! There is life in the river! Jump in the river today!

The River of God

In the river of God
There is joy!
There is life!
La fiesta hoy!

Jump in the river!
Come take a swim
Here you'll find cleansing
From all of your sin!

There's freedom in the river!
Come frolic and play
All you can eat
In this jubilation buffet!

Be like a child
Let go of reserve
Life to the full
No need to conserve!

The river is here
Beckoning to all
Live in the river
Hear the Lord's call!

☙ 36 ❧

And the seed that fell on good soil represents those who hear and accept God's word and produce a harvest of thirty, sixty, or even a hundred times as much as had been planted! (Mark 4:20 NLT)

One hundred fold! This is what the Lord wants for your life. Say to the Lord, "I want my life to bear maximum fruit for Your glory!" When you have good soil in your heart, this can be the result. Lord, bear one hundred fold fruit in our lives for Your glory!

One Hundred Fold

May my life
Bear one hundred fold!
Of spiritual fruit
Not of gold.

Making impact
In others' lives
Standing proudly
When Jesus arrives!

To live my life
For eternity,
Seeing with
Full clarity

This one life
Will soon be past
Hear my cry, Lord,
Of You I ask

One hundred fold fruit!
I want to bear
For Your glory
This is my prayer!

☩ 37 ☩

After a long time their master returned from his trip and called them to give an account of how they had used his money (Matthew 25:19 NLT)

Jesus is coming back! Are you ready for His return? Matthew 25 tells us about the Parable of the Talents, where the Master entrust His servants with His resources to invest them on His behalf. Then He returns, and the servants must give an account for how they stewarded the Master's resources. May you use all that He has entrusted you with wisely and generously for His Kingdom's advance!

The Return

Are you ready
For His Return?
He's coming again!
History adjourned!

King of Kings
And Lord of Lords
Bringing His
Eternal rewards.

We'll give account
On that great day,
Standing before Him
What will He say?

Well done My good
And faithful servant
You loved well
Your faith was fervent.

How I long
To hear those words
My life's goal
I'm undeterred.

✦ 38 ✦

But those who trust in the Lord will find new strength. They will soar high on wings like eagles. They will run and not grow weary. They will walk and not faint (Isaiah 40:31 NLT)

Soar with the Lord today! Mount up with wings like eagles. As you wait in His presence, the wind of His Spirit fills us your spirit with His power, love, and strength. You rise above your circumstances and look down with Him on your life. Seeing things from His perspective changes everything!

Soar

Soar to new heights!
Come ride on the wind
Go to the places
Where you've never been.

On wings like eagles
Soar with the Lord
Higher and higher
Pressing on toward

The high calling in Him
I run for the prize
Break out from the mundane
I now will arise.

Resurrection power
Fueling my heart
Higher and higher
I've been set apart

Come on, let's soar!
Join for the ride
There's room in His Heart
Where it's deep and wide!

✢ 39 ✢

"Sing, barren woman, you who never bore a child; burst into song, shout for joy, you who were never in labor; because more are the children of the desolate woman than of her who has a husband," says the Lord (Isaiah 54:1 NIV).

Sing it out! Sing the praise of the King! Praise to the King! He is great and worthy to be praised. When you sing to the Lord, you join heaven's chorus of angels and saints worshipping around the throne. When you sing, you welcome His presence and power into your life in a fresh way!

Sing It Out!

Sing it out!
Let out a shout!
What's inside
Let praise break out!

This is the time
To make some noise
To lay hold of
The Lord's new joys!

Joy of the Lord
Is my strength
Rising up
To a new wavelength,

Changing the
Whole atmosphere!
Breaking the
Stronghold of fear!

Sing it out!
Shout to the Lord!
People praising
In one accord!

✢ 40 ✢

*In the last days, God says, I will pour out my Spirit on all
people. Your sons and daughters will prophesy, your young men
will see visions, your old men will dream dreams* (Acts 2:17
NIV)

Pour out Your Spirit upon us, Lord! Just like in Acts 2! May the
Spirit of prophecy breathe on you and may you breathe out
prophetic declarations in the name of Jesus. May your nights be
filled with dreams from heaven, just like in the life of Joseph. And
may the Lord make those visions and dreams come to pass!

Visions and Dreams

I will pour out My Spirit
Upon all flesh
All weary souls
I will refresh!

Visions and dreams
Will come in the night,
I'll open your eyes
And give you My sight

To see what I see
To hear what I say
To do what I do
To follow My way

Dream a new dream
Like Joseph of old
See in advance
My plans will unfold

Living Acts 2!
In this day and age
Holy Spirit and I
On the same page!

✥ 41 ✥

So I will restore to you the years that the swarming locust has eaten, The crawling locust, The consuming locust, And the chewing locust, My great army which I sent among you (Joel 2:25 NKJV)

Our God is a God of restoration! He redeems, He restores. He makes all things beautiful in His time. Lord, show us the specific pains and traumas that we have faced in our lives. Take those very things and make something beautiful out of them. May they be places of healing and recovery for others!

Restore

I will restore to you
What locusts have eaten
Pains from the past
The times you've been beaten.

I make all things new
Make beauty from ashes
When I went to the Cross
And took all the lashes.

Brought wholeness to you
By My stripes you are healed
My Word has the power
My Sword you can wield.

Breaking down the lies
The strongholds that bind
When the enemy comes
I will remind

That in Me You overcome
That I will restore
All that you've lost
And so much more!

✢ 42 ✢

And I also say to you that you are Peter, and on this rock I will build My church, and the gates of Hades shall not prevail against it (Matthew 16:18 NKJV)

Jesus has been building His Church for the past two thousand years! Nothing will prevail against it. He gives you the privilege of joining Him in building His Church. His Church is not a building but people. You get to join Him in building lives that will impact the Kingdom for all eternity!

I Will Build My Church

I will build My Church
Upon this Rock
Confessing My name
I will grow My flock.

The gates of hell
Will not prevail.
Every scheme of the devil
Will surely fail.

My people released
To be salt and light,
Advancing My Kingdom
Making things right.

Proclaiming Good News
So needed today,
Telling the world
That I Am the Way.

So join Me in building
This great Church of Mine!
I'm with You always
Pour out the New Wine!

✧ 43 ✦

They asked each other, "Were not our hearts burning within us while He talked with us on the road and opened the Scriptures to us?" (Luke 24:32 NIV)

Enjoy the journey! You are on a journey of the soul with Jesus. Like the disciples on the road to Emmaus who were journeying with Jesus, may your heart burn within you as He gives revelation. He will complete the good work that He has begun in your life (Philippians 1:6). Enjoy the journey as the gift that it is!

Journey of the Soul

Journey of the soul
Come join for the ride!
With Jesus as our Captain
The very best soul guide!

Explore the deeper waters
Of your heart and soul,
Experience God's grace
Come and be made whole!

Healing and freedom
Is what you will find
As you plunge into the journey
Treasures will be mined!

Jesus is the Healer
The One who sets us free
He's our Destination
Opens possibility.

So join us on this journey,
The journey of the soul
Jesus take the wheel
Come and take control!

✢ 44 ✦

Therefore everyone who hears these words of Mine and puts them into practice is like a wise man who built his house on the rock. The rain came down, the streams rose, and the winds blew and beat against that house; yet it did not fall, because it had its foundation on the rock (Matthew 7:24-25 NIV).

Lord, build our lives upon the Rock! We want our lives to stand firm in the midst of whatever trial comes our way. We want to live lives of daily obedience. Our houses are built to last for all eternity!

Houses on the Rock

Houses on the Rock
Let's build a whole block!
Community of disciples
Walking the talk!

Hearing Jesus' words
Putting into action
The Kingdom on earth
Gaining real traction!

Rows and rows of houses
Let's take the whole city!
Letting the Light shine
Having no pity

On the devil and his schemes
Taking authority
God plus one
Is a majority!

Community of fire
Set ablaze for Him
Houses on the Rock
Let the building begin!

↭ 45 ↭

Now to Him who is able to do immeasurably more than all we ask or imagine, according to His power that is at work within us, to Him be glory in the church and in Christ Jesus through-out all generations, for ever and ever! Amen (Ephesians 3:20-21 NIV)

God, You are so much bigger than all we can ask or imagine! Break open our human limitations, our small understanding of who You really are. Show us in reality how big You are! May the world see and know that there is a Living God, the Creator of the universe who is also our heavenly Father!

BIG GOD!

God so much bigger
Than all of my fears
He's so much bigger
Than whatever appears!

Can do more than we ask
Or even imagine
In Him am content
In feast or in famine.

Break out of the box
That exists in my mind,
You're so much greater
You are unconfined!

No limitations
Omnipotent God
You parted the seas
When Moses lifted his rod!

On You I will focus
Big God on high
All of my worries
I gladly say goodbye!

✦ 46 ✦

I am the Alpha and the Omega, the First and the Last, the Beginning and the End (Revelation 22:13 NIV).

Our God is the Alpha and Omega, the First and the Last, the beginning and the end! He has all things in His hands. He is sovereign! You can fully trust in Him and place your life in His loving care. History belongs to Him. Glory to His name!

Alpha and Omega

Alpha and Omega
The First and the Last
Lord of the future
Lord of the past!

Lord of the present
You are the great I Am!
You are the Messiah
The Lion and the Lamb!

Omniscient in Your wisdom
So patient in Your love
So rich in Your mercy
I truly stand in awe of.

Holy, Holy, Holy
Lord God Almighty
The whole universe
Shines forth Your glory brightly.

Alpha and Omega
Beginning and the End
What is man that You
Would call us Your friends?

✢ 47 ✤

And He has made from one blood every nation of men to dwell on all the face of the earth, and has determined their preappointed times and the boundaries of their dwellings, so that they should seek the Lord, in the hope that they might grope for Him and find Him, though He is not far from each one of us (Acts 17:26-27 NKJV)

History is His story! The story of God. The story of man. The story of love. I was a history major at Berkeley and could see so clearly the hand of God in all that I learned there. Some of my fellow students could not and would not acknowledge the Lord in history. It was dumbfounding. I am so thankful to be part of His story. He calls you to call others to join in His story.

His Story

History is His story
The story of His love
Started in the garden
With man in the image of.

The God who wanted fellowship
To share and multiply
Loving one another
With God's full supply.

Then came the Fall
Where man said, "I am God."
"I'll do it on my own!
I think Your rule is flawed."

We broke the relationship
And broke our Father's heart
God sent His Only Son
To give us a new start!

His Story being written
In our lives today!
Immanuel, God with us
The Truth, the Life, the Way!

☙ 48 ☙

So from now on we regard no one from a worldly point of view. Though we once regarded Christ in this way, we do so no longer (2 Corinthians 5:16 NIV).

No longer see other's from a worldly point of view! You are called to see people with Kingdom eyes. With eyes of love, with eyes of faith. When Jesus first called Peter, He saw the Rock. When He called you and me, He saw us not only as we were but as what we would become. May you see others in the same way!

Kingdom Eyes

Help me to see
With Kingdom eyes
With revelation
To realize

That You are working
All around,
Drawing people
The lost are found.

Thru the chaos
Thru the trials
You are Sovereign
All the while.

Holy angels
Watching o'er me
Fighting battles
I cannot see.

Kingdom eyes
I see Your face
Everywhere
I see Your grace!

✤ 49 ✤

We are like common clay jars that carry this glorious treasure within, so that this immeasurable power will be seen as God's, not ours (2 Corinthians 4:7 Passion).

We are all jars of clay! We all have limitations and weaknesses. We are all jars of clay containing the great treasure of the Kingdom inside. May He increase; may we decrease. May His glory shine forth so bright for all to see!

Jars of Clay

We are all
Jars of clay
Treasure inside
We display.

Broken vessels
Marred by sin,
Redeemed by Jesus
Born again!

In our weakness
He is strong,
Little ones
To Him belong.

Trials and pain
Break us down,
We're made from dust
Came from the ground.

Jars of clay
Shine forth His light!
In this darkness
Glowing and bright!

✢ 50 ✦

*I am the Lord, who opened a way through the waters, making
a dry path through the sea* (Isaiah 43:16 NLT)

God will make a way for you! He parted the Red Sea; He delivered
Daniel from the Lion's den; He rescued Shadrach, Meshach, and
Abednego from the fiery furnace; He comforted Elijah in his
depression. He is the God who makes a way when there is no way.
Turn to Him, call on Him, surely He will make a way for you!

God Will Make a Way

God will make a way
When I'm at wit's end,
Have nowhere to turn
On Him I can depend.

He goes before Me
Preparing the way,
He's shaping me to be like Him
I am the Potter's clay.

I need to walk by faith
Trusting He's at work,
When I try to figure things out
My mind it goes berserk!

'Tis so sweet to trust in Him
He's proved me o'er and o'er
I belong to Him
I'm deeply loved and cared for.

God is making a way!
He is for you and for me,
Can't wait for what's in store
Can't wait for what we'll see!

FAITH

Then He touched their eyes and said, "Because of your faith, it will happen" (Matthew 9:29 NLT)

Faith plays such a key role in our relationship with God. The Bible tells us that "without faith it is impossible to please God" (Hebrews 11:6). Faith is heartfelt trust, which is essential in any healthy relationship. Faith played a big role in the healings of Jesus, where Jesus often directly in response to people's faith.

May these poems of faith inspire fresh faith in your hearts!

☙ 51 ❧

For we walk by faith, not by sight (2 Corinthians 5:7 NKJV).

Put on your faith glasses! Faith is the spiritual sight that you need to navigate through the journey of life. It is so tempting to see things only with your natural eyes, seeing only what your eyes can see. When you put on your faith glasses, you see the invisible and can do the impossible with God!

Walk by Faith!

Walk by faith
And not by sight,
Filled with courage
Rid of fright.

Seeing the
Invisible,
Doing the
Impossible!

Eyes are fixed
Upon Your face
Undistracted,
I'll run my race!

Pressing on
The upward way,
On higher ground
I'll watch and pray.

Blessed journey
This life of faith,
I am with You
The Lord sayeth!

✦ 52 ✦

But I say, "How can you show me your faith if you don't have good deeds? I will show you my faith by my good deeds" (James 1:18 NLT)

Brothers and sisters, let's walk our talk! St Francis of Assisi told us to "preach the Gospel, and if necessary to use words." Much needed counsel for believers today! This watching world needs to see believers loving one another and not clinging to our rights and our opinions. Lord, empower us to walk the talk!

Walk the Talk

Help me Lord
To walk my talk!
Lest I be full
Of poppycock!

Too many words
I hear today,
Not backed with action
The hollow way.

One word with action
Better than
A thousand promises
Without a plan.

Love is as
A Love that does!
He loved us first
That's our because.

Walk the talk
I will obey,
Faith in action
I will display!

❖ 53 ❖

But the Lord said to her, "My dear Martha, you are worried and upset over all these details! There is only one thing worth being concerned about. Mary has discovered it, and it will not be taken away from her" (Luke 10:41-42 NLT).

Worship the Lord and be worry free! When we worship God and fix our hearts and minds on Him, everything comes into proper perspective. We need not worry because our God is in control. He is fighting on our behalf. He is working all things together for our good. He is with us! Make the choice today to worship God and watch worry go by the wayside!

Worry or Worship?

Worry or worship,
Which will it be?
Worship the Lord!
Your soul is set free.

Worry says "I
Am the one in control"
In my world,
I play the title role.

Worship says, "He"
Rules and reigns on high.
I stand in awe
On Him I rely.

Worry weighs down
Worship lifts up,
Worry brings low
Worship fills your cup!

Worry or worship?
Come make your choice,
As for me and my house
We will rejoice!

✧ 54 ✧

There is salvation in no one else! God has given no other name under heaven by which we must be saved (Acts 4:12 NLT).

By grace, through faith, you are saved! Your salvation includes so much more than the forgiveness of sins! The word for salvation is *sozo* in Greek, and it includes healing, wholeness, and deliverance! This is all yours in your salvation! Lay hold of the full salvation that you have in Jesus!

Salvation

Salvation so much more
Than forgiveness of sins,
Salvation is a life
That begins when born again!

Purchased on the cross
The price that set us free,
Paid too for our healing
Foretold in Isaiah 53.

Salvation not just future
Though heaven is for real,
Salvation is now!
Jesus sealed the deal!

Working out salvation
With fear and trembling
Requires all our effort
To do the reassembling.

Salvation is here!
The Kingdom is at hand,
Taking hold today
Of the Promised Land!

✦ 55 ✦

I have said these things to you, that in Me you may have peace. In the world you will have tribulation. But take heart; I have overcome the world (John 16:33 ESV).

The ramifications of Easter continue on each and every day! Our risen Lord is with you, enabling you to live a life of resurrection power! You are called to live your life with a resurrection lens, seeing things from God's perspective.

Resurrection Lens

Though Easter weekend
Has come to an end,
I'll live my life
With a Resurrection lens!

Because He lives
I'll live too,
He is with me
In all I go through!

In this life
There will be trials,
Times are tough
Sometimes hostile.

I will not fear
I'll be of good cheer,
He's overcome
And He is near!

Resurrection lens
I wear each day,
The risen Lord
Leads the way!

⤜ 56 ⤛

"For My thoughts are not your thoughts, Nor are your ways My ways," says the LORD. "For as the heavens are higher than the earth, So are My ways higher than your ways, and My thoughts than your thoughts" (Isaiah 55:8-9 NKJV).

God's thoughts are higher than yours! You can rest in this truth. You can find comfort in this reality. You don't have to figure out everything. You don't have to understand everything. You just need to trust and obey for there's no better way!

Your Ways are Higher

As the heavens are higher
Than the earth below,
Your ways are higher
I can be still and know.

That You are God
You're in control,
This is the truth
No need for a poll.

In the midst of trouble
We will not fear
When things are uncertain
When vision's unclear.

Your ways are higher
You know what is best,
When I doubt
My faith's put to the test.

I trust in Your love!
Shown on the cross
No matter what circumstance
Of gain or of loss!

☙ 57 ❧

It is for freedom that Christ has set us free. Stand firm, then, and do not let yourselves be burdened again by a yoke of slavery (Galatians 5:1 NIV).

Freedom! There is freedom in the Lord. Jesus has set you free from sin, condemnation, fear. Hallelujah! May you live in the freedom that Christ has purchased for you on the cross! No more living in the shadows, there is freedom in the Lord!

Freedom (PART 1)

It is for freedom
That Christ has set me free,
So why this unseen force
Keeps its hold on me?

From within,
Fear grips my heart,
Fear of failure
Preventing me to start.

From without
What others say
Holds me captive
Their voice obey.

Fear not, You tell Me,
For I am here,
I AM greater
Than what you fear.

So I will trust
In what You say,
I'll walk on water
Amidst the fray.

✣ 58 ✣

Then you will know the truth, and the truth will set you free (John 8:32 NIV).

The truth will set you free! Before I met Jesus, I was so bound by self hate, pride, and addiction. I lived the opposite of a life of freedom. When I called on His name, He set me free—no more desire for drugs, no more living for the approval of people. Jesus set me free! Let Him set you free today!

Freedom (PART 2)

Egypt past
Canaan at hand,
Lord help me take
My promised land.

Dancing, soaring,
I rise above,
So free to be
The one You love.

Eyes on You
Your eyes on me,
Lost in Your
Reality.

Found by You
I now can breathe,
By Your Spirit
I do believe.

I can do all things
Through Christ in me,
By your grace
To simply be.

✦ 59 ✦

The fear of human opinion disables; trusting in GOD protects you from that (Proverbs 29:25 THE MESSAGE).

Break free from the fear of man! The fear of man is crippling—causing you to conform, to continually second guess your life. When you fear the Lord, He sets you free from the fear of man. You live before an Audience of One, who loves you and approves of you. You can be free to be the person that God has called you to be!

Freedom (PART 3)

Fear of man
Has been my snare,
Why so much
Of others care?

What they think
And what they say,
Their opinions
Holding sway.

Conforming to
What others want,
Disapproval
Is my haunt.

Christ has come
To set me free
From fear of man
Captivity.

I care now only
Of what He thinks of me.
I see His smile
And I am free.

✢ 60 ✢

But now, this is what the Lord says—He who created you, Jacob, He who formed you, Israel: "Do not fear, for I have redeemed you; I have summoned you by name; you are Mine. When you pass through the waters, I will be with you; and when you pass through the rivers, they will not sweep over you. When you walk through the fire, you will not be burned; the flames will not set you ablaze" (Isaiah 43:1-2 NIV).

Fear not! Fear is one of the greatest barriers in our lives—in everything. In your walk with the Lord, in your relationship with others. The Lord tells us again to "Fear not!" Yes, you don't need to fear—He is with you!! He will never fail you. He will help you get back up when you fall. He will strengthen you as you take new ground for Him! Fear not, my brothers and sisters!

Fear Not!

Fear not!
He's got
You in
His hands
By you
He stands
With you
He is
Always
You're His
No need
To fear
When He
Is near
Trust in
The Lord
Take up
Your sword!

✣ 61 ✣

For His anger lasts only a moment, but his favor lasts a lifetime; weeping may stay for the night, but rejoicing comes in the morning (Psalms 30:5 NIV)

The Lord turns our mourning into dancing! Life is filled with ups and downs. Times of mourning, times of weeping. Times of celebration. Times of rejoicing. The good news is that whether you are mourning or dancing, you are with Him!

Mourning to Dancing

Weeping lasts the night
Joy comes in the morning,
When will this pandemic end?
When is normal returning?

So much doom and gloom
So weary in this storm,
A whole year of madness
My spirit feels forlorn

I hold onto Hope in the midst
The anchor for my soul,
Nothing else will do in these times
Nothing else can fill the hole.

Watching, waiting for the hour
When morning will break through,
Until then I'll praise You, Lord
I put my trust in You.

Good things will come to all us
May hearts not grow faint!
Morning will come! I hear the sound!
The dancing of the saints!

✦ 62 ✦

Casting all your care upon Him, for He cares for you (1 Peter 5:7 NKJV).

Release outcomes to the Lord! Dallas Willard influenced my life in a very significant way. More than any other mentor I've known, Dallas truly lived out the reality of the Kingdom and exuded the character of Jesus through the very pores of his being. One of his most helpful teachings for me was about releasing outcomes to the Lord. When we can truly release outcomes to the Lord, then we can experience a worry free, peaceful life in the Kingdom.

Releasing Outcomes

Releasing outcomes
Lord set me free,
Giving my burdens
Over to Thee.

Thy Kingdom come
Thy will be done,
In my surrender
The battle is won.

Your yoke is easy
Your burden is light,
Living by faith
Not with my sight.

Whatever may come
You're in control,
I trust in Your goodness
I don't trust the polls.

I release all outcomes
Daily I repeat
Content in all things
In You I'm complete!

✦ 63 ✦

But seek first the kingdom of God and His righteousness, and all these things shall be added to you (Matthew 6:33 NKJV).

The God First life is the best life of all! When you put God as the first priority in your life, everything else will fall into place. God is worthy to be put in the highest place in your lives. He is faithful to keep His promises. He loves you with a perfect love that casts out all fear. Our God is an awesome God!

The God First Life!

The God First life
Is the life for me!
Seeking first His Kingdom
Wholeheartedly.

All other things
All other people
Cannot compare
God has no equal.

All spiritual games
I will put aside,
Laying down completely
The idol of my pride.

Living life in union
With my First Love,
Over all else
God comes above.

Lord, I pledge to live
The God First life
All other idols
Killed with Abraham's knife!

✦ 64 ✦

But be doers of the word, and not hearers only, deceiving your-selves (James 1:22 NKJV).

Just do it! I think James (not Lebron or Nike) came up with the original "Just Do It" slogan. What a great call for believers to simply live out our faith! We have too many words. We need to just simply be the salt and light that we have been called to be, without any fanfare. Brothers and sisters, let's just do it!

JUST DO IT!

Too much talk!
Too many words!
JUST DO IT!
No more action deferred!

Show me your faith
By loving the poor
By loving the one
Who lives next door!

Show me His love
By fighting injustice,
The powers that be
No longer must dis!

The image of God
That's in everyone!
Redeemed by His blood
Loved by the Son.

JUST DO IT!
JUST DO IT NOW!
Let's write a new chapter
Hands to the plow!

✦ 65 ✦

Instantly something like scales fell from Saul's eyes, and he regained his sight. Then he got up and was baptized (Acts 9:18 NLT)

The blinders and scales need to come off! When Ananias prayed for Paul, scales fell off his eyes. The scales of religion, self righteousness, pride... Whatever hinders your clear vision of the Lord Jesus are scales that need to fall from your eyes. Lord, remove our scales that we can see You as You are in Your glory!

Scales Are Falling

Scales are falling
From my eyes,
Exposing all
The devil's lies.

Like Apostle Paul
On the road,
Living by
Religious code.

One encounter
Changed it all.
The pride crashed down
Scales did fall.

When Light comes in
Darkness leaves,
Now I am able
To perceive.

The Kingdom is real
It's close at hand,
In His Kingdom
I make my stand.

✢ 66 ✢

In the beginning God created the heavens and the earth. Then God said, "Let Us make human beings in our image, to be like Us. They will reign over the fish in the sea, the birds in the sky, the livestock, all the wild animals on the earth, and the small animals that scurry along the ground" (Genesis 1:1, 26 NLT).

Our God is the Creator God! He created the heavens and the earth. He created you and me. When He simply spoke, "Let there be light," light came into being! You have been created in the image of your Creator God. You have been created to be a creator. Part of being an image bearer is to manifest His creativity in our world.

Creativity

Breathe on me, Lord,
Your Creativity
Created in Your image
From dust into 3-D!

Created the heavens and earth
Created all living things
Created summer and the fall
The winter and the spring!

Spirit hovering o'er waters
Resting in my soul,
Waiting to give birth
Your beauty will unfold.

Speaking forth Your words of life
Calling things that are not
As though they were into being
The power of Your thoughts!

Anoint me Lord by Your Spirit
With Your creativity
That I may live outside the box
In Your activity!

✦ 67 ✦

Then God said, "Let there be light," and there was light. And God saw that the light was good (Genesis 1:3-4 NLT).

God said, "Let there be light and there was light"! Think about this awesome and amazing fact. Our God is awesome in power; there is none like Him. Ask Him to shine His light upon your life, your heart today. Darkness will flee; it cannot stand in the presence of our God, who is light!

Let There Be Light!

God spoke His word
Let there be Light!
All the darkness
Suddenly became bright!

Shekinah glory
Emanating from God,
In His presence
We are all awed.

Let His light shine
On the earth today,
Opening eyes
Showing forth His way.

Shining into hearts
Warmth from the Son,
Melting bitterness
Hate's day is done.

Let there be Light!
We declare it today
May it be so
In Your name, we pray!

✧ 68 ✦

There's a young boy here with five barley loaves and two fish.
But what good is that with this huge crowd? (John 6:9 NLT)

God wants to do a fresh miracle in your life! Bring your five loaves
and two fish to the Lord today and see what miracle He will do.
He is the same yesterday, today, and forever. Don't focus on your
lack; focus on His miracle working power!

Five Loaves and Two Fish

Five loaves and two fish
All that He needs
To make a miracle,
Multitudes He feeds!

A little boy's lunch
Was the offering,
Jesus blessed it
In doing so watering

The seed that was sown
Was multiplied,
Showing His glory
Known worldwide.

What do you have?
Your loaves and two fish!
Bring them to Jesus
Make a holy wish.

Lord, take what I have
And use it for You.
Can't wait to see
What You will do!

✥ 69 ✥

And I will do whatever you ask in My name, so that the Father may be glorified in the Son. You may ask Me for anything in My name, and I will do it (John 14:13-14 NIV).

Jesus has given His disciples access to use His name! When you pray in the name of Jesus, He will answer you! What an amazing authority and power that you have access to. May you pray with boldness and confidence for the sick to be healed, for the lost to be saved! Thank You, Lord, for giving us access to Your name!

Power in Your Name

There's power in Your name
Your Kingdom we proclaim
You've overcome the grave
You've broken every chain!

In Your name there is life
In Your name there is power
In Your name there is healing
Your name is our strong tower.

Lord, we come right now
Asking in Your name,
Yesterday, today, forever
Jesus, You're the same!

The God who did miracles
Does them all today,
The blind will see, the lame will walk
And demons will obey.

Lord, we praise Your name!
Lift up Your name on high!
Jesus You are worthy
Love personified!

✤ 70 ✤

"Lord, if it's You," Peter replied, "tell me to come to You on the water." "Come," He said. Then Peter got down out of the boat, walked on the water and came toward Jesus (Matthew 14:28-29 NIV).

Jesus calls you to get out of your boat! To leave your comfort and to walk on the water—today! He is the same yesterday, today, and forever. Yes, it's scary to leave your boat, but what an amazing adventure He calls you to! Peter would never have walked on water if he didn't get out of his boat. Same for you today. Be courageous and get out of the boat!

Come Out of the Boat

If it's You, Lord,
Tell me to come
To walk on water
I won't succumb

To the waves
Or wind in fear,
I'll come to You
As You draw near.

I'll leave my boat
My comfort zone.
I'll fix my eyes
On You alone.

I'll leave familiar
Things behind
Into the unknown
New adventure I'll find.

Lord, I hear
Your call to come
Invitation
To everyone!

✦ 71 ✦

Jesus looked around and saw them following. "What do you want?" He asked them. They replied, "Rabbi" (which means "Teacher"), "where are You staying?" "Come and see," He said. It was about four o'clock in the afternoon when they went with Him to the place where He was staying, and they remained with Him the rest of the day (John 1:38-39 NLT)

Come and see! Jesus invited the first disciples to check Him out, to see for themselves if Jesus was worth following. To see Him in action, to hear His Words, to experience His heart. After spending time with Jesus, they were convinced. This invitation to "Come and see" stands today. See for yourself this Jesus who has forever changed the course of human history.

Come and See

Come and see
Come take a look
At the One
Who's in the Book.

Come and see
For yourself,
Put the hearsay
On the shelf.

He changed my life
He'll do the same
For everyone
Who calls on His name.

Jesus Christ
The same today
Tomorrow and
Yesterday.

Come and see
You won't regret!
He's offering
A life reset!

⤏ 72 ⤎

Then He said to them all: "Whoever wants to be My disciple must deny themselves and take up their cross daily and follow Me" (Luke 9:23 NIV).

The same call to discipleship that Jesus gave 2000 years ago stands today! Salvation is free; discipleship is costly! Dying to self and taking up our cross is a high cost and calling. It is also totally freeing. For when you do so, you are free to be the person He has called you to be!

Come After Me

If anyone would
Come after Me,
You must deny yourself
Take up your cross daily.

No other way
To be found,
The way of discipleship
No longer bound!

By the world's attachments
The world's false pleas,
We are cured
From sin's disease!

Life with Me
Is truly the best,
Give Me a try
Put Me to the test.

Come after Me
Be set free!
Know the truth
And live abundantly!

☙ 73 ❧

"Come now, and let us reason together," says the Lord, "Though your sins are like scarlet, they shall be as white as snow; though they are red like crimson, they shall be as wool" (Isaiah 1:18 NKJV).

The Lord calls you to love Him with your mind! He calls you to reason with Him. Presenting your life to Him is your reasonable worship (Romans 12:1). Ponder and think about the Lord and the promises He gives to you. Following Jesus is the most sensible and reasonable decision you can ever make!

Come Let Us Reason

Come let us reason
Let's think things through,
Align with My Word
Your mind I'll renew.

Seeing the end
From the beginning
Will save you regret
Will keep you from sinning.

See from up higher
From My point of view,
Seek out My wisdom
How I long to guide you!

Love Me with Your mind
Your heart and your soul,
Critical thinking
Will help you unfold

My plans for you life
Are good and are best,
Come let us reason
Come and be blessed!

✦ 74 ✦

*Enter through the narrow gate. For wide is the gate and broad
is the road that leads to destruction, and many enter through it.
But small is the gate and narrow the road that leads to life, and
only a few find it* (Matthew 7:13-14 NIV).

Enter through the narrow gate! The pathway to discipleship begins
with entering through the narrow gate, a turnstyle for one. Can't
enter as a group. The life of discipleship is the life that says no to
the philosophies and values of the world and says yes to the
Kingdom. It's often difficult and unpopular. Yes, Lord, we will
follow You on the narrow way!

The Narrow Gate

Enter thru the narrow gate
The path that leads to life.
The broad road leads to death
It's filled with envy and strife.

The entrance is narrow
Enter one by one,
The turnstile opens
When you believe in the Son.

Jesus is the Gate
The Gate that leads to freedom,
Reigning with the King
In His righteous Kingdom.

Like swimming against the stream
Going against the grain,
The narrow way is hard
But there's so much to gain!

So enter in today!
Thru the Narrow Gate
Let your life begin
Salvation activate!

⇥ 75 ⇤

Jesus replied, "If I want him to remain alive until I return, what is that to you? As for you, follow Me" (John 21:22 NLT)

Jesus has given you a clear example to follow! Not only that, He Himself is your personal guide to lead you step by step in your life! He is your map and guide! Praise God! You just need to stay close, following His leading each and every day of your life. He can be fully trusted! Follow Him wholeheartedly!

Follow Me

Take up your cross
And follow Me,
Keep your eyes fixed
Undistractedly!

Don't follow the world
And all of its ways
For life's more than money
Life's more than play.

Don't look to the left
Don't look to the right
Walking by faith
Not walking by sight.

I've set the pattern
Shown you an example,
I've given you power
That's more than ample.

Follow Me now
No more delay,
Blessings await
For those who obey!

✦ 76 ✦

Let us then approach God's throne of grace with confidence, so that we may receive mercy and find grace to help us in our time of need (Hebrews 4:16 NIV).

You have unlimited access to the very presence of God! When Jesus died on the cross, the curtain that blocked the Holy of Holies was torn in two—meaning you now have free access to God. It is at God's throne that you can find all the mercy and grace that you need to live a life of abundance. Hallelujah!

Approach the Throne

Come with boldness
Approach the throne,
He's waiting gladly
For we're His own.

Finding mercy
Finding grace,
In time of need
He'll always embrace.

No condemnation
No fear here!
He'll always forgive
Will always hear.

When we call
Upon His name,
He'll remove our guilt
Take away shame.

When Jesus died
On Calvary,
Access was granted
Permanently!

↭ 77 ↫

Deep calls to deep in the roar of Your waterfalls; all your waves and breakers have swept over me (Psalms 42:7 NIV).

Deep calls out to deep! The deepest part of your soul cries out to connect to the deep heart of God. Only in Him can you find satisfaction—the love you need. The great news is that when you call upon Him, He hears you and answers! So call on Him today, for He will hear and answer your cry!

Deep Calls Out to Deep

Deep calls out to deep
My soul cries out to You,
Longing for connection
Needing a breakthrough.

Buried in my heart
Found beneath my mask,
The true me is waiting
Waiting to be asked.

Where are you? You say
Come out from your hiding,
No more pretending
No more backsliding.

Here I am, my Lord,
Just as I am I come
Without one plea, unashamed
Back to where I'm from!

Deep connects to Deep!
I've found myself in Thee
So loved and secure
My soul's jubilee!

❖ 78 ❖

Then He said, "Go out, and stand on the mountain before the Lord." And behold, the Lord passed by, and a great and strong wind tore into the mountains and broke the rocks in pieces before the Lord, but the Lord was not in the wind; and after the wind an earthquake, but the Lord was not in the earthquake; and after the earthquake a fire, but the Lord was not in the fire; and after the fire a still small voice (1 Kings 19:11-12 NKJV).

How we need to hear the still, small voice of the Good Shepherd! In the midst of the noise in the world and in your mind, take time to be still before Him. Ask Him to speak. He will. His sheep know His voice. He wants to speak to you in a personal and powerful way!

Still Small Voice

Your still small voice
I want to hear,
Whispering to me
You are near.

This is the way
Walk ye in it,
Step by step
And bit by bit.

Like Elijah
In the cave,
Rest and refreshing
Your Spirit gave.

Peaceful sound
Your still small voice,
When I hear
I make the choice

To follow You
Wherever You lead,
In surrender

I've been freed!

⊹ 79 ⊹

Therefore if anyone cleanses himself from the latter, he will be a vessel for honor, sanctified and useful for the Master, prepared for every good work (2 Timothy 2:21 NKJV)

You have been set apart for the Lord! Set apart from the world, to be holy and cleansed from the things that are not in alignment with His Kingdom. Set apart for the Master's purpose. Your life is to be used for His glory and to make a great impact for His Kingdom! To God be the glory!

Set Apart

I'm set apart
For You, Lord.
All others things
I cut the cord.

One thing I ask
One thing I seek
To see Your face
To hear You speak.

Lord, my life
Belongs to You.
You saved my soul
You made me new.

Here I am, Lord,
Send me now,
To Your will
I gladly bow.

I'm set apart
For you, Lord.
Life with You
I'm never bored!

✦ 80 ✦

Jesus said to him, "I am the way, the truth, and the life. No one comes to the Father except through Me" (John 14:6 NKJV).

Jesus is THE Way, THE Truth, and THE Life. Not a way, a truth, and a life. This is a tough truth in the relativistic milieu of our day. Jesus' words stand today. There is no other way to the Father but through Him. Praise His name for giving you this solid ground to base your life upon!

The Way, Truth, and Life!

While we await
Our country's fate,
Counting the votes
My teeth start to grate.

Watching the news
Hour by hour,
Country divided
The mood is sour.

Where can we turn?
In whom can we hope?
Who can save us?
Send us a rope?

I hear His whisper
Calling to us,
"Come unto Me
In Me put Your trust!"

I am the Answer
To all of your strife
My name is Jesus
The Way, Truth, and Life!

⇸ 81 ⇷

There is one body and one Spirit, just as you were called in one hope of your calling; one Lord, one faith, one baptism; one God and Father of all, who is above all, and through all, and in you all (Ephesians 4:4-6 NKJV)

We stand on the common ground of our faith in Jesus! We may have differences of opinion regarding politics and minor points of theology, but we are ONE in Christ. Let's lay aside our differences and come together on our common ground, showing the world our unity in Christ.

Common Ground

Blue AND Red
Left AND Right,
Common ground
The cross in sight.

Biden and Trump
They're mere men,
Not the hope
For those born again.

Jesus is First
Priority
He's our final
Authority.

Common ground
We find in Christ,
All are called
To sacrifice.

We stand on Him,
Christ our Rock.
All together

As ONE flock!

⇥ 82 ⇤

The time is fulfilled, and the kingdom of God is at hand. Repent, and believe in the gospel (Mark 1:15 NKJV).

The Kingdom of God is at hand! The reign of God is here! You simply need to repent and believe. Repent from your ways and your desire to be in control, believe in the Lord and put your trust in Him. It's as simple as that. When you repent and believe, you can live in the reality and power of God's Kingdom!

Rain/Reign of God!

Holy Spirit, rain on me
Like a gentle shower
Soften up my hardened heart
Fall down in this hour.

Of chaos and fear, these troubled times
How we need Your reign!
Defeating the defeated foe
His attacks are in vain.

Times of refreshing needed here!
Rain of God pour down!
Saturate me with Your love
In You I will abound.

Jesus come, rule and reign!
You are the King of Kings
No other name, higher than Yours
Lord of everything!

When the rain/reign of God comes down
Everything's alright!
All things are possible
With Your power and might!

⇸ 83 ↤

Now I am about to go the way of all the earth. You know with all your heart and soul that not one of all the good promises the Lord your God gave you has failed. Every promise has been fulfilled; not one has failed (Joshua 23:14 NIV).

God is faithful! We recently celebrated the Garden Church's 25th anniversary. My wife, Sharon, and I planted the church when we were both twenty-five years old. God has truly proven Himself as faithful to us and to our church family. It was a joyous time of celebration and giving God glory for His goodness. It is so important to reflect, remember, and celebrate how the Lord has worked in our lives! Do so today!

Twenty-five Years

Looking back,
Our spirits smile.
You've been with us
all the while.

Leading, working,
Your Spirit guides.
On our hearts
You have transcribed

Faith. In the One
Who never fails,
Putting wind
Into our sails.

To move forward
Chapter two,
Impossible
Is nothing to You.

Heaven bound
We're having fun,

The best is yet
To surely come!

☀ 84 ☀

The One who calls you is faithful, and He will do it (I Thessalonians 5:24 NIV).

The Lord has a personal calling for each one of our lives! You must seek Him wholeheartedly to discover His calling. When He reveals His calling to you, then you must give your all to it. You find true purpose, meaning, and fulfillment in fulfilling His calling!

Calling

Help me, Lord
To know Your calling,
As times goes by
I find myself stalling.

Getting caught up
In worldly affairs,
Heart is divided
Weighed down with cares.

Before I was born
In my mother's womb,
You loved me and knew me
Over me did croon.

The Father's song
The Father's love
Pouring down
From heav'n above.

Release me, Lord
To do Your will
With my life
I will fulfill!

✢ 85 ✣

Blessed are those who hunger and thirst for righteousness, for they will be filled (Matthew 5:6 NIV).

Lord, may we hunger and thirst after You, after Your Kingdom! May we not hunger for the things of the world. Lord, increase our spiritual hunger that we may be satisfied in You, causing an even greater hunger and a greater filling!

Hunger and Thirst

Those who hunger and thirst
Will surely be filled.
Only You can satisfy
In You I'm fulfilled.

When I hunger for the world
And fall for the devil's tricks,
My spirit starts to wilt,
My soul becomes sick.

How my soul craves
The sweet Bread of Heaven
Pure and delightful
Rid of all leaven.

Thirsty for You,
The Living Water,
Given freely
To Your sons and daughters!

Filled to the brim!
Overflowing with joy
Jesus, You're amazing!
You're the Real McCoy!

LOVE

We love because He first loved us (1 John 4 :19 NIV).

God is love! We love God, and we love one another because we know and experience the love of God. It starts with Him! He is the initiator of love. May these poems of love be a catalyst for the fresh experience of the love of God in our hearts. And in response, may we love Him and love one another with all of our hearts!

✝ 86 ✝

So the young son set off for home. From a long distance away, his father saw him coming, dressed as a beggar, and great compassion swelled up in his heart for his son who was returning home. The father raced out to meet him, swept him up in his arms, hugged him dearly, and kissed him over and over with tender love (Luke 15:20 Passion)

Receive the Father's love! Experience today His love in a fresh way. Let Him hug and kiss you, welcome you into His arms, and shower you with His love. Our heavenly Father is crazy about you. Don't let anything separate you from the Father's love. Open your heart to Him: His heart is wide open towards you. Run into His arms.

The Father's Love

The Father's love
Has greater reach
Covering over
Every breach.

Running to us
With open arms
His hugs and kisses
Will disarm.

Our defenses
And our shame
We are His own
We bear His name.

Reckless love
Coming after me,
His healing love
Has set me free.

In the Father's love
I am home
Where I am loved
And I am known.

⭢ 87 ⭠

So now I am giving you a new commandment: Love each other. Just as I have loved you, you should love each other. Your love for one another will prove to the world that you are my disciples (John 13:34-35 NLT).

Love one another! Obeying this command will change the world. Love is the most powerful force in the universe. Jesus calls us to unleash this power by loving one another as He has loved us. This love will bring healing, restorations, renewal, and revival to our world. Our love for one another is the greatest witness that we can give to the world!

The New Command

On the eve of the Cross
Just as He planned,
He told His disciples
The new command.

Love one another
As I have loved you
I laid down My life
Lay down yours too.

Sacrificial love
Shown on the cross,
The flavor of the Kingdom
It's true secret sauce.

By this all will know
That you belong to Me,
Known by your love
For the whole world to see

Crystal clear
Is the new command
To love one another
This is the Jesus brand!

✢ 88 ✢

I pray that they will all be one, just as You and I are one—as You are in Me, Father, and I am in You. And may they be in Us so that the world will believe You sent Me (John 17:21 NLT).

Father, make us one! On the night that Jesus went to the cross, He prayed for all His disciples—that we would be one. He then went to the cross to die for all our sins—our sins of rebellion, hate, racism, pride. At the foot of the cross, we all are on level ground. In these divided times, may we answer our Lord's Prayer for unity and truly love one another!

Father Make Us One!

Father make us One
Answering Jesus' prayer
That the world would know we're His
The love of Christ we wear.

United in the Kingdom
Living for the Lord
Black, White, Yellow, Brown
Living in one accord.

Overcoming differences
Forgiving each other's wrongs
By the blood of Jesus
To His family we belong.

Doing Kingdom justice
Fighting for the oppressed,
Taking up our cross
Love's our litmus test

In these divided times
We must come together,
Brother, sisters, we are one!
We are His living letter!

☙ 89 ❧

And surely I am with you always, to the very end of the age
(Matthew 28:20 NIV).

The Lord Jesus is with you always! 24/7! 365 days a week! This promise is so comforting and reassuring. You are never alone. You never have to figure life out on our own. You never have to go through challenges and struggles by yourself. He is with you! Rejoice!

I Am With You Always

I am with you always
'Til the very end,
Won't leave or forsake you
How I love my friends!

My peace will be with you
I'll guide you day by day,
With Me you're never lost
Walking on the way.

My presence is your comfort
In times when life gets hard,
I am your protection
I am your Rear Guard.

My fragrance is upon you
Filling up the air,
Freshening up the world
Without any fanfare.

I am with you always!
Rest in me today
24/7!
I'm with you all the way!

✦ 90 ✦

Won't You revive us again, so your people can rejoice in You?
(Psalms 85:6 NLT).

Restore my passion, Lord! As you reflect on Jesus' sacrificial love
for you, may it become fresh in a personal and intimate way. Let it
go deep into your soul and melt away all the clutter—bitterness,
double mindedness, and worldliness. The Lord will release the
fresh fire of passion in your heart today!

Restore My Passion

Restore my passion, Lord
Often it leaks,
Longing for intimacy
Your face I seek!

As I reflect
Upon the cross,
All my gains
I count as loss.

All other things
I put aside,
I humble myself
And kill my pride.

I love you Lord
Because You first loved me,
You are my
Top priority.

Restore my passion
Send Your Holy fire,
In my heart today
May my flame grow higher!

✦ 91 ✦

Yet I am confident I will see the Lord's goodness while I am here in the land of the living (Psalm 27:13 NLT).

God is good all the time! All the time, God is good! I love that greeting we sometimes use in church. It is so true! God is good! All the time! Even in our times of trouble, He is good! He is with you, making all things work together for the good of those who love Him and are called according to His purpose (Romans 8:28). God is good all the time!

God Is So Good

God is
So good
Anything
He would

Do to
Show you
His love
Is true.

Sent His
Only Son
The cross
For everyone.

Greater love
Has none
Our hearts
He's won.

Say yes
To Him
New life
Will begin!

❖ 92 ❖

But He said to me, "My grace is sufficient for you, for My power is made perfect in weakness." Therefore I will boast all the more gladly about my weaknesses, so that Christ's power may rest on me (2 Corinthians 12:9 NIV).

Weakness is strength! Paul's perspective on weakness and suffering is so comforting and encouraging. You can glory in your weaknesses, not hide or run from them. You can glory in them because they are an opportunity for you to experience the power and grace of our Lord Jesus in your life. Without the weaknesses, you would feel less need for God in your life. With them, you are drawn to Him and will truly know that His grace is sufficient for you!

Strength in Weakness

Strength in weakness
My secret in life
Surrendering to God
Letting go of my strife

When I am weak
Then I am strong
God's grace covers me
When I am wrong

When I admit
My dependency
I overcome
My tendency

To take control
To take the wheel
To press forward
In fleshly zeal

Such freedom I've found
As I yield to You
Strength in weakness
You pull me through!

☙ 93 ❧

And yet, O Lord, you are our Father. We are the clay, and you are the potter. We all are formed by your hand (Isaiah 64:8 NLT).

Welcome to the Potter's Wheel! Heavenly Potter, we welcome Your hand of shaping and forming in our lives. We long to be conformed into the likeness of Christ. Take away the things in our lives that do not reflect who You are and who we are in You. Though painful, we welcome Your shaping in our lives. We love You, and we trust You, Lord. Use our lives for Your glory!

The Potter's Wheel

The Potter's Wheel
I'm in His care
He's shaping me
Making repairs.

In my soul
The broken parts
Healing wounds
Deep in my heart.

He's molding me
To be like Him
Taking off
My dragon skin.

Bringing forth
The hidden things
Deep desires
Find their wings.

The Potter's Wheel
The place to be
Making dreams
A reality!

✦ 94 ✦

You will keep in perfect peace all who trust in you, all whose thoughts are fixed on you! (Isaiah 26:3 NLT)

Perfect peace! A gift from the Lord that He freely gives to us, again and again! Because of what He has done for us on the cross and because of His presence with us, we can truly say, "It is well with my soul."

It Is Well

It is well with my soul
Because the well inside
The Living Water flows
The river deep and wide.

No matter what befalls me
I'm content in Him,
I have learned the secret
In the Kingdom gym.

Trusting in His Promise
When I can't see the way.
Holding onto Jesus
My fears, they are allayed.

Thru the darkest valley
Thru the deepest night,
Your rod and staff they comfort me
I'm gonna be alright!

Soul, it is well with you
For you belong to Him.
Thru the cross I know
That in the end we win!

✦ 95 ✦

They brought the donkey and the colt to him and threw their garments over the colt, and he sat on it (Matthew 21:7 NLT).

Our Lord is a humble King! One of the striking, beautiful traits of our Lord Jesus is His humility. This is clearly seen in the Triumphal Entry, when Jesus entered into Jerusalem on a donkey heading straight for the cross. He is God, yet He is a humble servant. He didn't ride on a fancy chariot; He rode on a humble donkey. O come let us worship, let us adore our humble King!

Triumphal Entry

Riding on a donkey
Jesus, the humble King
The shouts of Hosanna
Crowds loudly cheering.

Headed to the cross
The King came to die,
The Suffering Savior
His love is the why.

The crowds would soon turn
Call to crucify,
Falsely accuse
Sentence to die.

For this Jesus came
To take on our sin,
The weight of the world
Falling on Him.

At this Triumphal Entry
Let's ponder the One
Who laid down His life
Our hearts He has won!

✢ 96 ✢

When the Roman officer who stood facing Him saw how He had died, he exclaimed, "This man truly was the Son of God!" (Mark 15:39 NLT)

Come to the cross! There is a powerful spiritual called "Were You There" that has made a deep impact on me. The first two lines go: "Were you there when they crucified my Lord? Oh! Sometimes it causes me to tremble, tremble, tremble." Reflect upon the cross and what Jesus underwent there for you and for me so that we could be forgiven. So that we could be free. Salvation is free, but it is not cheap. Surrender your life once again to the One who laid down His life for you.

Were You There?

Were you there my friend
When they crucified our Lord?
The nails in His hands
The piercing of the sword?

Unspeakable agony
Our Lord went through
For you and for me
To secure our rescue.

Greater love
Has none than this
To not receive
We'd be remiss.

Look to our Savior
Nailed on the cross,
I lay down my pride
I'm at a loss.

For words, I worship
Humbly bow down,
At the Cross
Your Grace Abounds!

⊹ 97 ⊹

*When He had received the drink, Jesus said, "It is finished."
With that, He bowed His head and gave up His spirit* (John
19:30 NIV).

It is finished! The work of redemption and reconciliation has been
completed on the cross! Hallelujah! Thank You, Jesus, for loving us
in such a tangible way. We can never doubt Your love for us when
we look at the cross. Nothing needs to be added to Your work of
the cross! Our striving is finished, our human efforts to be made
acceptable to You are finished. We rest in the redemption found in
the cross!

It Is Finished!

It is finished!
It is done!
Sin defeated
The battle won!

Jesus' death
Upon the cross
Defeated Satan
And his weak sauce.

Paid in full
My debt forgiven,
Now I'm on to
Abundant livin'.

Jesus nailed
Upon the tree,
Freedom for all
Who will believe.

It is finished!
It is done!
This salvation
For everyone!

⊹ 98 ⊱

Jesus replied, "You must love the Lord your God with all your heart, all your soul, and all your mind" (Matthew 22:37 NLT).

You are invited to have a two-way, wholehearted love relationship with the Living God! The Lord calls you to this amazing intimacy with Him. Often because of fear, we hesitate to give ourselves wholly to the Lord. What is the solution? To experience His love for you in a fresh way. When you experience this love that surpasses knowledge (Ephesians 3), you can respond to the Lord in a wholehearted way, without reserve. May you experience His wholehearted love today and may you, in turn, love God with true wholeheartedness!

Wholehearted

Help me to live
With my whole heart,
Self preservation
Must depart.

To live with gusto
No regrets,
To give my all
Turn on the jets!

To live for God
To live with God
To live wholehearted
For His applause.

To give to God
My everything
My joy, my pains
To Him I bring.

Wholehearted is
The way He loves me!
Wholehearted is
The way I love Thee!

✣ 99 ✣

Then the Lord God called to the man, "Where are you?"
(Genesis 3:9 NLT)

Come out from hiding! In the Garden, when Adam and Eve
sinned, their relationship with God was broken. Father God came
seeking to restore the broken relationship. He asked the tender
question, "Where are you?" Adam and Eve were filled with shame,
covered themselves with figs, and tried to hide from their heavenly
Father. The same scenario is present today. Our heavenly Father
asks you the question, "Where are you?" inviting you back to a
loving relationship with Him. Respond to His call and be
reconnected with your Loving Father!

Where Are You?

In the beginning
Our Father asked,
Where are you?
Take off your mask.

Naked, ashamed
And filled with fear,
Hiding, covering
As God drew near.

Come back to Me
I'll cover you
With these skins
From animals I slew.

A picture of
The cross of Christ
Where Jesus died
A sacrifice

Where are You?
Come back to Me
Reconciled
And fully free!

✧ 100 ✧

*And a voice from heaven said, "This is my Son, whom I love;
with him I am well pleased"* (Matthew 3:17 NIV).

We are His beloved sons and daughters! With you He is well
pleased! This needs to go deep into your heart and soul. This is
your identity in God. With this identity firmly intact, you can do
all things through Christ who gives you strength.

Who Am I?

"Who am I" is the question
That all of us ask.
Who is the me
Buried behind my mask?

Defined by the world
By what others think,
Always adjusting
We live on the brink.

Of coming undone
Imposter syndrome,
Who will rescue me?
Am I all alone?

I am His beloved!
I am His dear child.
When God first looked at me,
I know that He smiled!

I am secure
In my identity,
For I know that I'm loved
I'm free to be me!

✤ 101 ✦

We love because he first loved us (1 John 4:19 NIV).

Your love is a response to His love! Your love for Jesus was not initiated by you; it is a response to His love. This is Love—Jesus laying down His life for you. You are loved fully and completely! As you receive His love deep into your heart, respond by loving Him with all of your heart! Lord Jesus, we love you!

We Love Because He First Loved Us

We love because
He first loved us,
It was at the cross
Where we hopped on Love's bus!

While we were yet sinners
Christ died for us,
Demonstrating His love
Turned our minus to a plus!

God took the first step
Showing His love,
This is His nature
What He is made of.

We then love Him
And we love one another,
We are one family!
Sisters and brothers!

Receive His love afresh
Coming from above,
Flowing to and through us
Agents of His Love!

⁜ 102 ⁜

Oh, what joy for those whose disobedience is forgiven, whose sin is put out of sight! (Psalms 32:1 NLT)

O happy day! When Jesus washed our sins away! Because of Jesus' death on the cross, you are fully forgiven and free. Your sin debt has been paid; you are now cleansed by His blood and restored to intimate relationship with Him! Rejoice in the forgiveness that He has given to you!

I Am Forgiven

I am forgiven
My sins are washed away
By the blood of Jesus
O happy day!

He took my sin upon Him
He took my very place,
Now that I'm forgiven
The devil has no case.

No more condemnation
No more life of fear,
My chains have been broken
I'm living in the clear!

Because I've been forgiven
Others I forgive,
It's the cycle of grace
In God's love we live.

Do you need forgiveness?
Call upon His name
He will surely answer
You'll never be the same!

✧ 103 ✧

Then Peter came to Him and asked, "Lord, how often should I forgive someone who sins against me? Seven times?" "No, not seven times," Jesus replied, "but seventy times seven!" (Matthew 18:21-22 NLT)

Unlimited forgiveness! Given to you, you must give to others. This can only be done by plugging into the grace of God. In your human ability, you cannot offer unlimited forgiveness to others; it is too difficult. But when you draw upon the unlimited forgiveness of our heavenly Father, you can give away what you have received from Him! Is there anyone in your life that you need to forgive today? Ask the Lord for His help and His resources so you can offer His gift of forgiveness to others.

Seventy Times Seven!

Seventy times seven?
How can this be?
Unlimited forgiveness
When others sin against me?

Impossible task
With human strength alone,
This can only happen
When we come to His throne.

And receive His forgiveness
Given so freely,
Then we offer to others
What's been given to me.

Forgive us our debts
As we forgive our debtors,
You taught us to pray
So we can live better.

For power and strength
Look to the cross
Where Jesus forgave us
And paid the great cost!

✦ 104 ✦

He has shown you, O mortal, what is good. And what does the Lord require of you? To act justly and to love mercy and to walk humbly with your God (Micah 6:8 NIV).

The Micah 6:8 mandate is the call to love our neighbor as ourselves. It is so needed in the divided, distressed times that we are living in. Believers in Jesus, it is time to speak out on behalf of the oppressed…to speak out against systemic racism…to speak on behalf of the unborn…to care for those who are suffering. What a better world it will be as we live our Micah 6:8 in our daily lives!

Micah 6:8

He has shown you, O man
What is truly good,
Clear life instructions
Easily understood.

To live your life justly
To care for the oppressed,
This is a faith that's lived
Not just confessed.

To live loving mercy
With compassion in your core,
Loving our neighbors
Helping to restore.

To walk humbly with your God
To bear the easy yoke
To deal gently with others
Even when you're woke.

Let's heed the call of Micah
Lord let Your Kingdom come
Marching in one accord
To the heavenly drum!

✧ 105 ✧

Jesus wept (John 11:35 NIV).

Jesus was human like us; He cried real tears—tears of compassion, tears of empathy. May the Lord give you His tears as you encounter the pains of others. May your heart know His heart. And may your hands move in conjunction with His hands. These tears will bring healing in the lives of others.

TEARS

Give me Your tears, Lord
Let my heart break
With the things that break Yours
Let my soul ache.

So much brokenness
And pain all around,
Tears flow like rivers
Watering the ground.

To see what You see
To feel what You feel,
To Your grace and mercy
I do appeal.

Tears that will water
The hardness of my heart,
To enter people's pain
To not live apart.

Give me Your tears, Lord
I will not look away,
Loving the hurting
This is what I pray.

⤜ 106 ⤛

Even though I walk through the valley of the shadow of death, I will fear no evil, for You are with me; Your rod and Your staff, they comfort me (Psalm 23:4 ESV).

In these difficult times we are living in, we are NEVER ALONE! Jesus' very name, Immanuel, reminds you that He is with you always. In Him is peace, power, protection, provision, and perfect love!

Never Alone

Through the deep valley
I am never alone,
You're always with me
You are my home.

When I feel weak
You give me strength,
When I cry out
You'll go to any length

To rescue me
Again and again.
When I fall into
The lion's den.

Your yoke is easy
Your burden is light,
Following You
My path is bright.

Hallelujah!
I'm never alone!
Immanuel,
You call me Your own!

110

✤ 107 ✤

Give all your worries and cares to God, for He cares about you (1 Peter 5:7 NLT).

The Lord cares for you! Personally. Wholeheartedly. You have Someone you can go to with your heavy burdens, worries, and stresses. You can give your cares to Jesus, and He will help you. Thank You, Lord. We bring all of our cares to you today and find fresh encouragement and strength in You!

Cast Your Cares

Cast your cares
Upon the Lord.
He'll hear your cries
You're never ignored.

A faithful Friend
Who bears our burden,
Who comforts us
Time and again.

A mighty God
Who moves in power,
Our weakness is
The perfect hour.

For Him to show us
His love and grace,
For Him to know us
Face to face.

He cares for you
He cares for me.
So cast your cares
And be set free!

⤞ 108 ⤝

Therefore, it was necessary for Him to be made in every respect like us, His brothers and sisters, so that He could be our merciful and faithful High Priest before God. Then He could offer a sacrifice that would take away the sins of the people (Hebrews 2:17 NLT).

The Son of God, the second Person of the Godhead, became a man! He knew what it was to be thirsty, hungry, happy, and sad. He experienced the full range of human emotions. He knows what it is to be just like us but without the sin. Therefore, He can identify with us, and we can identify with Him. We can find comfort and strength in this awesome reality!

Just Like Us

Jesus became a man
Just like us
Yet was without sin
So we can fully trust.

That He knows what we feel
He knows what it's like
He felt the pain
When He took the spikes.

Jesus knows hunger
Jesus knows thirst
Jesus knows joy
Knows us at our worst.

What a friend we have
In Jesus our Lord
Through knowing Him,
We are restored.

Just like us!
Our Savior became
He died on the cross
We're saved in His name!

✦ 109 ✦

So now I am giving you a new commandment: Love each other. Just as I have loved you, you should love each other. Your love for one another will prove to the world that you are My disciples (John 13:34-35 NLT).

Dr. Martin Luther King had a vision of the "Beloved Community." Dr. King envisioned it as a society based on justice, equal opportunity, and love of one's fellow human beings. Dr King's vision of the Beloved Community comes from THE KING, our Lord Jesus Christ. May we heed this call of Dr. King and the King of Kings, our Lord Jesus, in this day of trouble in the land.

Beloved Community

A beloved community
Where we LOVE one another,
Living in unity
As sisters and brothers!

A society based
On equal opportunity,
No matter your color
A space you can freely be.

A place filled with justice
Where all people's rights
Are defended and valued
For this we all fight.

Dr. King's vision
Was the same as THE KING's,
The Kingdom of God
Shalom will bring.

By this all will know
That we belong to Him,
That we're His disciples
That we are ALL KIN!

✤ 110 ✤

Where there is no vision, the people perish (Proverbs 29:18 KJV).

Dr King's vision of love is so needed in our day! He was a Christ follower, and got His vision from Christ. This is what we need to be known for—our love for one another. Loving not just our neighbors, but our enemies too! It is this love that overcomes the world.

Remembering MLK

This day we remember
Dr. Martin Luther King,
A prophet to our nation
Shouting, "Let Freedom Ring!"

Love conquers hate
Right prevails o'er wrong,
We shall overcome
Join the Kingdom song!

Calling for equality
For justice in the land!
Calling for believers
To ALL take a stand!

A beautiful dream
Where everybody wins,
Where people are not valued
By the color of their skin.

Let's all heed his words
In this time of division
Let's live in unity
Fulfilling his great vision!

⥲ 111 ⥺

Come to Me, all you who are weary and burdened, and I will give you rest. Take my yoke upon you and learn from Me, for I am gentle and humble in heart, and you will find rest for your souls. For My yoke is easy and My burden is light (Matthew 11:28-30 NIV).

Come to Me! This is one of the most appealing, incredible invitations in all of the Bible! Jesus calls you to come to Him, to lay down all the weights and heavy burdens that you are carrying! To REST! To be with Him, to learn from Him. The easy yoke of Jesus is not a luxury, it is a necessity for living!

Come to Me

Come to Me
All those weighed down
By heavy burdens
Breaking you down.

I'll help you carry
Your heavy load,
My yoke is easy
On the narrow road.

Learn from Me
I'm humble and gentle,
I'm not condemning
Or judgmental.

Rest you'll find
When You come to Me,
It can't be bought
My grace is free.

Come to Me
Come right now
Life abundant
I'll show you how!

→ 112 ←

For God so loved the world, that he gave his only begotten Son, that whosoever believeth in him should not perish, but have everlasting life (John 3:16 KJV).

Salvation is for all who believe! Jesus' invitation to each and every person on the planet stands today. Respond to His personal invitation! Invite others to respond to the invitation. John 3:16 is sorely needed Good News to our weary and broken world!

Whosoever Will

Whosoever will
Believe in the Son
Will have eternal life
Call on Me, it's done.

John 3:16
The greatest news on earth,
Declaring to all people's
Their tremendous worth.

That God would give His Son
As a ransom for us all,
To give us a life do over
An extreme overhaul.

God so loved the world
Demonstrated His love,
Died on the cross
Showed what His heart is made of.

This invitation it stands
For whosoever will
Call on His name
Your life He will fill!

✣ 113 ✣

The steadfast love of the Lord never ceases; his mercies never come to an end; they are new every morning; great is your faithfulness (Lamentations 3:22-23 ESV)

God's mercies are new every morning! As the Israelites collected the manna daily for forty years in the wilderness, so you can receive and gather the fresh mercies falling from heaven each day! Jesus taught us to pray, "Give us this day our daily bread." Take hold of His fresh mercies today!

Mercy Is Falling

Mercy is falling
All around,
Everywhere
It can be found!

Mercies new
And mercies old,
Mercy God does
Not withhold!

Falling down
Into my heart,
Never-ending mercy
Won't depart.

Lift up your hands
Unto the Lord,
Catch His mercy
Being outpoured.

Mercy is falling
On us all!
Taking home
A mercy haul!

⊹ 114 ⊱

So he returned home to his father. And while he was still a long way off, his father saw him coming. Filled with love and compassion, he ran to his son, embraced him, and kissed him (Luke 15:20 NLT).

We are melted by the compassion of the Father! When we are at our worst, His compassion shines the brightest. Welcoming us. Embracing us. Putting the best robe on us and a ring on our finger. Receive the compassionate embrace of our compassionate God. Extend that same compassion to others.

Compassion

The father of the prodigal
Felt it flowing through his veins,
As he saw his son
Broken and in chains.

The shepherd felt it too
When sheep 100 was lost,
He left the ninety-nine
To find it at all cost.

May compassion be the fuel
The feeling in my heart,
The love that Abba has for me
To others to impart.

I wanna care for others like Jesus cares for me
The song we sing it goes
More than words or sentiment
More than flowery prose.

Lord, may this year of serving others
Be simple and succinct,
Actions prompted by Your love
Write with Spirit ink!

✢ 115 ✦

Her children arise and call her blessed; her husband also, and he praises her: "Many women do noble things; but you surpass them all." Charm is deceptive, and beauty is fleeting; but a woman who fears the Lord is to be praised. Honor her for all that her hands have done, and let her works bring her praise at the city gate (Proverbs 31:28-31 NIV).

Without our moms, we would not be here! My mom went to be with the Lord in 2007, and there has been a hole in my heart ever since. I thank God for my mom and her godly influence in my life. She was a worshipper who loved God with all of her heart. Her heart and legacy of worship has passed to me as it is my greatest passion. Love you, Mom! Will see you soon in heaven!

Thank God for Mothers!

Here is a tribute
To the moms of the world
From the moment they said
It's a boy! It's a girl!

From day one
You have cared for our needs
From making us breakfast
To plugging nosebleeds

Always you're giving
Always you care
Always forgiving
And willing to share

We want to say THANK YOU!
From bottom of heart
God's face shine upon you
His blessings impart

Mothers we love you!
We thank God for you
Not only on Mother's Day
All other days too!

119

⊹ 116 ⊱

What a person desires is unfailing love (Proverbs 19:22 NIV).

We were made for love—to be loved and to love. Our God is Love (1 John 4:8). He is the source of love. People will disappoint and fail. Not God, His love is perfect. His perfect love casts out; we find freedom in His love!

Perfect Love

Perfect love
We all search for,
Not found on earth
We keep knocking on doors.

Where can we find
This perfect love?
We've looked everywhere
Now let's look above.

To the One
Who is Perfect Love,
Our empty hands
Meet their glove!

Filling our hearts
Setting us free,
Making us whole
Your love is the key!

God's perfect love
Driving out fear,
Jesus, my valentine
My heart now is seared!

✦ 117 ✦

When he finally came to his senses, he said to himself, "At home even the hired servants have food enough to spare, and here I am dying of hunger! I will go home to my father" (Luke 15:17-18 NLT).

The prodigal son had a moment of clarity that was a game changer. He came to His senses! How much better it is to be in the Father's house! We just need to humble ourselves and return! If you are a prodigal and have left the Father's house (like we all have), come home today! The Father is waiting for you!

Come Home!

In these tense times
We all need more laughter.
We need it now
Not just in the hereafter.

So much anger all around
Division and strife,
The tension so thick
Can be cut with a knife.

We all need to breathe
Take time to exhale.
We need a reprieve
Fresh wind in our sails.

Who can refresh me
Bring me a new smile?
The Father of the prodigals
Is waiting all the while

For us to come home!
It's warmer inside
Let's come to our senses
And lay down our pride.

✦ 118 ✦

And from the overflow of his fullness we received grace heaped upon more grace! (John 1:16 Passion)

I love the beach! The beach reminds me of God's grace, wave after wave of grace pouring over our lives. Take time in God's nature— you will find God there! The beauty of His creation draws us closer to Him!

I Love the Beach!

I love the waves
Pounding the shore,
Reminds me of grace
There's always more.

I love the sounds
Water rushing in,
Whitewashed sand
The beach's skin.

I love the smells
Of the sea,
Ocean's atmosphere
Filling me.

I love the people
Walking by,
Each one loved
By God Most High.

I love the beach!
My favorite place
To soak in God's
Amazing grace!

✦ 119 ✦

Out of the ground the LORD God formed every beast of the field and every bird of the air, and brought them to Adam to see what he would call them. And whatever Adam called each living creature, that was its name. So Adam gave names to all cattle, to the birds of the air, and to every beast of the field (Genesis 2:19-20 NKJV).

From the beginning, there was a special relationship between man and animals. Animals were created by God to live in harmony with mankind. I lost my best friend dog, Chopin, to cancer last year. I experienced so much of God's grace and love through my furry friend. So thankful for the years we had together.

Man's Best Friend

Tough day at work
And then I come home.
Chopin's there to greet me
And throw me a bone!

Of unconditional love,
Licking my face.
Dogs are the best
Furry models of grace!

Always so happy
To be by my side,
Always on my team
His loyalty's bonafide.

Chopin is a warrior
Always guarding our pack,
Chasing coyotes
Anything for a snack!

Sadly it's the time
To say my farewell
Chopin, how I'll miss you!
In my heart you'll always dwell!

☙ 120 ❧

Yet a time is coming and has now come when the true wor-shipers will worship the Father in the Spirit and in truth, for they are the kind of worshipers the Father seeks. God is spirit, and his worshipers must worship in the Spirit and in truth (John 4:23-24 NIV).

We are called to worship God in Spirit and in truth. To worship Him with all of our hearts with full passion. And to worship Him with our minds, with greater understanding of who He is. May the Lord send fresh fire upon our worship, so that our worship in Spirit and in truth may be like fresh incense ascending to heaven.

In Spirit and in Truth

In Spirit and in truth
I worship God Most High,
He's worthy of my praise
Ten thousand reasons why.

With all of my heart
I'll hold nothing back,
Such a Good Shepherd
There's nothing that I lack!

With all of my mind
I try to grasp His Ways,
You're sovereign in love
You're with me all my days.

Taste the Living Water
Gives life to your soul,
The woman at the well
Drank and was made whole.

Lord we heed the call
Worshippers arise!
In this Kairos time
Hallelujah reprise!

About the Author

David Kim is senior pastor at The Garden Church. He is a passionate worshipper and has been a faithful shepherd of God's people at The Garden since 1995. He earned his Master of Divinity and Doctorate of Ministry degrees at Fuller Theological Seminary. He is married to his college sweetheart, Sharon, and is the proud father of sons Daniel and Joel.